CHINA'S CENSORSHIP OF THE INTER-NET AND SOCIAL MEDIA: THE HUMAN TOLL AND TRADE IMPACT

HEARING

BEFORE THE

CONGRESSIONAL-EXECUTIVE COMMISSION ON CHINA

ONE HUNDRED TWELFTH CONGRESS

FIRST SESSION

NOVEMBER 17, 2011

Printed for the use of the Congressional-Executive Commission on China

Available via the World Wide Web: http://www.cecc.gov

U.S. GOVERNMENT PRINTING OFFICE

72–895 PDF   WASHINGTON : 2012

For sale by the Superintendent of Documents, U.S. Government Printing Office
Internet: bookstore.gpo.gov   Phone: toll free (866) 512–1800; DC area (202) 512–1800
Fax: (202) 512–2104   Mail: Stop IDCC, Washington, DC 20402–0001

CONGRESSIONAL-EXECUTIVE COMMISSION ON CHINA

LEGISLATIVE BRANCH COMMISSIONERS

(II)

CONTENTS

CHINA'S CENSORSHIP OF THE INTERNET AND SOCIAL MEDIA: THE HUMAN TOLL AND TRADE IMPACT

THURSDAY, NOVEMBER 17, 2011

Congressional-Executive
Commission on China,
Washington, DC.

The hearing was convened, pursuant to notice, at 10:08 a.m., in room 2226, Rayburn House Office Building, Representative Chris Smith, Chairman, presiding.

Also present: Senator Sherrod Brown; Representative Tim Walz.

Also present: Harry Wu.

OPENING STATEMENT OF HON. CHRIS SMITH, A U.S. REPRESENTATIVE FROM NEW JERSEY; CHAIRMAN, CONGRESSIONAL-EXECUTIVE COMMISSION ON CHINA

Chairman SMITH. The Commission will come to order.

I want to welcome all of our distinguished witnesses to this very important hearing. We really appreciate the attendance of all of our panelists and guests. It's a pleasure to welcome everyone to this important hearing on "China's Censorship of the Internet and Social Media: The Human Toll and Trade Impact."

As recent events have shown, the issue of Internet censorship has only grown in terms of importance and magnitude, and I thank the Congressional-Executive Commission on China's staff for organizing a hearing on this pressing issue and for the tremendous scholarly work they have done not only in presenting our annual report, which is filled with facts and information that is actionable, but for the ongoing work that they do to monitor the gross abuses of human rights in China.

As the Congressional-Executive Commission on China's report demonstrates, China's leadership has grown more assertive in its violation of rights, disregarding the very laws and international standards that they claim to uphold while tightening their grip on Chinese society.

As Chinese citizens have increasingly called for freedoms and reforms, China has only strengthened its controls over the many areas of society, particularly over the Internet. While China has witnessed a boom in the popularity of social media and Internet sites, China's citizens that access online sites today remain under the watchful eye of the state. By some accounts, China has imprisoned more Internet activists than any other country in the world, and its Internet invariably ranks among the most restrictive globally.

Chinese citizens are unable to voice a range of criticism that Americans undoubtedly take for granted each and every day. Chinese citizens that Tweet about local corruption may face the threat of abuse or harassment. Citizens that express dissatisfaction over tainted food supplies that injure children, the most vulnerable population of our society, may come to hear a knock at the door. And citizens that voice the yearning desire for democracy and right to protections we value so dearly may disappear into the official custody of the state, where they face torture and incarceration.

For Chinese citizens, the line that can't be crossed is unclear. While mentions of the 1989 Tiananmen protests are surely prohibited, China's censorship remains at the whims of governmental agencies that seek to limit any of what they perceive to be destabilizing commentary. In China, the Internet provides no transparency and citizens must weigh their choices each time they click to send an email, or press a button, or post personal views.

Who can forget Shi Tao, who for merely posting information about what he's not allowed to do with regard to Tiananmen Square, garnered a 10-year prison sentence when Yahoo! opened up their personally identifiable information and gave it to the Chinese secret police that led to his conviction. There are no lists of banned words, as we know. There are no registers of prohibited topics. It's all kept secret. In China, there is no transparency and there are only consequences, and dire ones at that.

Today we welcome two panels that will address China's Internet censorship from two perspectives. The witnesses will not only provide personal accounts of how China's censorship affects individuals and families, but also detail how China's actions hinder the rights of U.S. businesses that seek to compete fairly in the People's Republic of China. These panels will expose China's bold disregard for its own laws and its international obligations, specifically in terms of its controls on Internet activity and expression.

In the first panel today we will hear personal accounts of the consequences Chinese citizens face in seeking to express their fundamental right of expression. We will hear from a son and a pastor that have seen firsthand the actions of an unforgiving hand of China's Internet police. We will hear how the simplest calls for freedom and reforms lead to the separation of loved ones and the partition of families.

In the second panel we will hear how China's Internet restrictions and controls not only hurts its citizens, but also hurts countries seeking to better China through international trade and cooperation. On a commercial level, China simply lacks the kind of transparency and fairness that we expect in global trading partners.

China has not only failed to comply with its WTO commitments, it has exploited our expectations to create an unlevel playing field, hurting the competitiveness of U.S. businesses and workers alike. We recognize that the Internet and social media can and should be used to provide people with greater access to honest information and to open up commercial opportunities for businesses operating in global markets.

We know that the promise of information technology cannot be achieved when it is used by repressive governments to fine, capture, convict, and so often torture ordinary citizens for voicing concerns publicly. Information technology cannot be advanced when it involves the systematic exclusion of commercial competitors in rampant disregard for transparency and intellectual property.

China is one of the most repressive and restrictive countries when it comes to the control of the Internet and the impact goes far beyond the commercial losses of U.S. companies that want to participate in that market. There are serious human rights implications. We have seen the damage inflicted countless times through the arrest of bloggers and pro-democracy activists who have used the Internet to communicate with colleagues or disseminate views and then have been arrested.

What makes this situation even worse is that sometimes it is U.S. companies, and my colleagues will recall I held the first of a series of hearings where we had Microsoft, Yahoo!, Cisco, and Google before our committee. It was my Subcommittee on Human Rights. They held up their hands and promised to tell the whole truth and nothing but, and then said they couldn't tell us what they were censoring and would not tell us how they were being complicit.

Harry Wu was here, and obviously has been a leader in that. He pointed out that Cisco has so enabled the secret police to track down people using Police Net, and that the use of cyber police is ubiquitous throughout all of China in order to capture the best and the bravest and the smartest in China who would bring that country to democracy, if only allowed to do so.

So this hearing will focus on these very important issues. We are joined by, obviously, our Cochairman, Senator Brown, Sherrod Brown from Ohio, who will speak, and then Mr. Walz, who is the Ranking Member, and then we will go to our witnesses.

[The prepared statement of Representative Smith appears in the appendix.]

STATEMENT OF HON. SHERROD BROWN, A U.S. SENATOR FROM OHIO; COCHAIRMAN, CONGRESSIONAL-EXECUTIVE COMMISSION ON CHINA

Senator BROWN. Thank you, Mr. Chairman. Thank you all for being here. It is an honor to have you. Pastor Zhang, thank you. And Alex Li, who goes to one of Ohio's great universities, Bowling Green State University, located in a small town outside Toledo. Alex got here at 4 o'clock this morning after riding a bus all night. Thank you for your extraordinary effort to get here. You can do that at your age and not pay a price like the rest of us, riding all night. But thank you. You look great today. Thanks.

Chairman Smith, thank you. Chris and I have worked together when I was in the House in the 1990s and into the next decade on China human rights issues. I am so appreciative of the work that he's done. And Tim Walz, who has been a stalwart on this Commission and on these issues, having lived in China many years ago for a while and taught there for a couple of years. Thanks for the work that you're doing.

The business of the Internet and social media is changing the way the world works. Just take a look at all the smart phones in this room. It has changed the way we live, the way we do business, the way we act as a society. It's changed the world. It's made people closer in many ways to their governments. It's made these governments more accountable and interactive. In the case of the Arab Spring, it's helped to topple dictators.

The purpose of today's hearing is to shed light on the darkness of China's repressive Internet and social media censorship. It's a policy that takes a human toll, as Chairman Smith said, undermining human rights freedoms and freedoms of expression and speech. It's a policy that's unfair to U.S. trade interests, especially for U.S. tech companies.

It's well documented that Chinese officials block access to far too many Web sites, including this Commission's. Some sites are blocked because they're considered politically sensitive, others for reasons that we could only guess. China's Internet control forces private companies, including U.S. companies, to censor the Internet based on vague and arbitrary standards.

Many companies are forced to operate in an opaque world that we know surprisingly little about. This policy benefits Chinese domestic companies at the expense of companies like Facebook, Twitter, and YouTube, who are completely blocked in China. Companies whose business models rely on openness and transparency are forced to be an arm of the Chinese Government or to turn their backs on 1.3 billion customers.

But it is not just Silicon Valley companies that are blocked, it's also companies in my State, like GrafTech and Edgetech that risk having their Web sites blocked or disrupted as they try to sell their services and products to reach Chinese consumers.

When a company goes public with complaints about these restrictions, as Google did last year, they risk retaliation by the Chinese Government for doing so. Google is a company that made the unfortunate controversial—and some decision that many of us weren't wild about—to work with the Chinese Government. In the end, of course, it didn't work out so well for them.

In the absence of meaningful competition, copycat versions of Twitter and Facebook flourish in China and raise hundreds of millions of dollars, ironically, on our capital markets. For instance, in May of this year, Renren, China's version of Facebook, raised $743 million in an IPO listed on the New York Stock Exchange. These Chinese companies are beholden to the Chinese Government and Communist Party and censorship has increased, yet they want access to our free and open society.

As arms of the Chinese Government, these moves should be closely scrutinized. China now has over half a billion Internet users, more of course than any country in the world. Most of these Internet users are young, far more aware of Chinese and world developments than their parents. Knowledge and openness are threats to totalitarian regimes. We know that. The Chinese Government knows that.

In our country, knowledge and openness are pillars of our form of government. Take the case of outspoken dissident/artist Ai Weiwei. His savvy social networking skills and unabashed criticism of the government landed him an 81-day detention at a secret location earlier this year. Now the government wants him to pay $2.4 million in alleged unpaid taxes and penalties by Tuesday. Thousands of supporters in China have sent him money over the Internet.

Ai continues to defy government orders by using Twitter to publicize his case. In recent years, the Commission has documented a growing number of cases of political imprisonment involving the Internet. Behind each case is a story and a family. One of those cases is Li Yuanlong. Li is a journalist who was imprisoned for two years for criticizing the Communist Party online. That's why we're so grateful that Alex, his son, is here to tell Li's story.

Last month, the U.S. Trade Representative filed a request for information from the World Trade Organization on China's Internet censorship. I applaud this move as a positive first step. I look forward to learning what we can do to address this pressing issue. Too much is at stake. The human toll becomes insufferable. The economic threat undermines our innovation.

China plays by its own rules because we regrettably, in this institution and in our government, let them. We cannot simply wait out the inevitable power of the Internet to move the hearts and minds of the Chinese people. We must do all we can to shine a light where free expression, thought, and commerce are too often kept in the dark.

Thank you, Mr. Chairman.

Chairman SMITH. Thank you, Mr. Chairman.

Mr. Walz?

[The prepared statement of Senator Brown appears in the appendix.]

STATEMENT OF HON. TIM WALZ, A U.S. REPRESENTATIVE FROM MINNESOTA; RANKING MEMBER, CONGRESSIONAL–EXECUTIVE COMMISSION ON CHINA

Representative WALZ. Well, thank you Chairman Smith and Senator Brown. It's an honor to be up here with two of the most passionate and thoughtful members of Congress, and I appreciate the long work that the two of you have done to bring about human rights, to bring about a sense of fairness, and today is another example of that.

I would also like to thank the witnesses for being here. It is very humbling to be on this Commission because the witnesses who sit in front of us are people that have paid heavy prices for freedoms, not just in China but worldwide, to make us understand those precious liberties we have. The folks in front of us today are no exception.

To Alex and his father who paid a price for that, we all benefit from that courage. We all benefit from keeping in mind that human rights are above and supreme to the other issues at hand. But I'm also very appreciative of the second panel here, a group of experts to help us understand the impact of what's happening with social media, and also understanding how it's impacting markets. It is our responsibility, as Senator Brown said, for this institution to uphold the human rights as well as trade deals that were signed onto.

Our companies are being unfairly punished by the behaviors of the Chinese Government and that is what this Commission was set up for. That was the mandate that this Commission was given, and I can tell you that my two colleagues sitting up here take that very seriously. So I look forward to the testimony today. Again, thanks to the witnesses. I always make sure I say this here. I am always incredibly impressed with the staff of this Commission. They are the most professional and best prepared of any I've seen, and I thank them.

So, Mr. Chairman?

Chairman SMITH. Mr. Walz, thank you very much. Thank you for the expertise you bring to this Commission, especially having lived there and having gotten to know the on-the-ground situation in China. You are a great asset to our Commission, so thank you.

We'll begin with our two witnesses on the first panel. We'll begin with Alex Li, who is currently an undergraduate student at Bowling Green State University in Bowling Green, Ohio. In 2006, a Chinese court sentenced Li's father, Li Yuanlong, to two years' imprisonment for posting comments online about the Communist Party. Then we'll hear from Pastor John Zhang, who is a rights advocate who was imprisoned for two years following the 1989 Tiananmen Square protest. Pastor Zhang currently assists families of political prisoners and serves as a pastor at California Bay Area Church.

Mr. Li, if you could proceed.

STATEMENT OF ALEX LI, COLLEGE STUDENT AND SON OF LI YUANLONG, WHO SERVED TWO YEARS IN PRISON FOR COMMENTING ON THE COMMUNIST PARTY ONLINE

Mr. LI. Greetings. My name is Muzi Li. I'm from Bowling Green State University. In 2005, my dad had published four articles online and was arrested because he published four articles online. At that time I was 17 years old. A few weeks after my dad was arrested I was brought to a hotel and questioned by the police from the Ministry of Public Security. I was questioned without a parent with me. One of the questions was, "What did your father do with your email address at omegacepearee@hotmail.com?" Nothing. Nothing. But according to the verdict, my dad published four articles through my email address. That was wrong. Why? The police say my dad published the articles through my email address. That's the case.

At that time my computer was operating a Windows XP system. I would just use the Windows Live to watch more news and the account number was totally omegacepearee@hotmail.com. It's not an email address, it's an account number. The police tracked my IP address and then the account number showed up. They thought it was an email address, but it wasn't. So they thought my father published those articles through the email address, but my dad didn't.

So it was all the Golden Shield. The police cannot track my IP address and they cannot find the account number. So according to the verdict, my dad used my email address, but that was wrong. So I think that proved that the police tracked my IP address through some technology and they used the Golden Shield to arrest those who have opposed political voices, and that happened to my family.

At that time I was 17 years old, a teenager. I was choosing a college. I needed my father, but he was taken away. So I think this was totally a tragedy. Moreover, when my dad committed these articles for a foreign Web site, and if somebody wants to publish something on a foreign Web site, what he needs to do is copy, paste, and post. An email address is not necessary. However, even if my dad needed an email address, he has his own. Why did he use mine? It's ridiculous. So the police tracked my IP address through technology and my dad suffered two years in prison. I also suffered two years without my father with me. That's the story.

Chairman SMITH. Mr. Li, thank you so very much.

Mr. Zhang? Pastor Zhang?

STATEMENT OF JOHN ZHANG, CHRISTIAN POLITICAL DISSIDENT IMPRISONED FOR TWO YEARS FOLLOWING THE 1989 TIANANMEN PROTESTS AND WHO CURRENTLY ASSISTS FAMILIES OF CHINESE POLITICAL PRISONERS

Mr. ZHANG. Ladies and gentlemen, thank you very much for holding this hearing. My name is John Zhang. I am currently a pastor in the Bay Area of San Francisco.

Twenty-two years ago in 1989, I was a student at the Beijing Language Institute. I actively participated in the 1989 Patriotic Democratic Movement in Beijing. After the Tiananmen Square incident, I organized a large memorial service to mourn for the Beijing residents and university students who were massacred at Tiananmen Square, and was arrested on June 15. I was arrested and sent to Qincheng prison in Beijing for two years.

In 2001, I was baptized as a Christian. Soon after, I became a house church preacher in an underground house church. Every Sunday I led dozens of Christians to hold Sunday worship at hotels, restaurants, and at the houses of some Christian followers. In 2004, on the eve of the 15th anniversary of June 4, I was arrested again. Why? Because I tried to organize an evangelism and invited many dissidents by phone or via email to attend our church's worship, but my phone was bugged and email was hacked by policemen, so I was once again illegally detained by the policemen and taken into custody for 10 days.

In 2006, I thanked God for bringing me to America, where I attended theological seminary and got my master's degree after three years' study.

Today, I just want to introduce a girl to everybody. This is Chen Qiao. Her English name is Bridgett. Her father, Liu Xianbin, is a famous Christian dissident in China. When she was only two years old, her father was taken away from her life. So her father disappeared from her life for nine years. When she was 11 years old, her father appeared in her life, but he felt like a stranger. She is 14 years old now. But she only lived with her father only less than four years. In her adolescence, she needed her father most. But unfortunately, her father was sent to jail for 10 years. This is the third time he was sent to jail.

So I think the American company Cisco has played a disgraceful role in this sad story. According to the reports, Cisco helped China's Ministry of Public Security construct the "Golden Shield Project" as well as provided equipment, technology, and training. The "Golden Shield Project" is a national surveillance network system that has a huge database and a sophisticated tracking network system. Policemen can track dissidents' IP addresses and then track, harass, and arrest them. I saw this in four articles published on Cisco's Chinese Web site, clearly showing the cooperative relationship between Cisco and China's Ministry of Public Security. Without a doubt, Cisco is responsible for the deterioration of Internet freedom in China. I hope that the Commission will enter these documents into the record.

Today, I just want to remind everyone that freedom of speech is an inherent right given to man by God, which is an inalienable right. The United States was established on the values of Christianity. The United States should defend and adhere to these universal human values and promote "non-evil" business practices. Each Member of Congress has the responsibility to monitor American companies like Cisco while trying to maximize the business interest in China. These companies should not ignore the most basic morals and principles of business ethics. In order to regulate the business practices of companies that violate American law, they should be subject to public criticism, condemnation, economic penalties, and sanctions.

Thank you for your patience.

[The information appears in the appendix.]

[The prepared statement of Mr. Zhang appears in the appendix.]

Chairman SMITH. Pastor Zhang, thank you so much for your testimony and for bearing witness to an extremely troubling truth in China, the mistreatment of house pastors, the mistreatment of all people of faith who are not registered and, to a large extent, co-opted by the government.

I would note parenthetically that Frank Wolf and I, right before the Olympic Games, traveled to China with the express hope of meeting with a number of religious leaders, including underground pastors. Every one of them, except one, was arrested, denied, precluded the opportunity to meet with two visiting Members of Congress.

Second, the one who did meet with us for dinner was subsequently arrested and interrogated very severely. So I thank you for bearing witness for fellow pastors and other men and women of faith in China who suffer daily, and now with the increased or the enhanced use of surveillance provided by the Internet.

And Mr. Li, thank you as well for your testimony.

All of us thought we might ask a question or just make a brief comment, and then we'll get to our second panel. If I could, were you in Beijing Prison Number One, by the way, Pastor? Which prison were you held in after Tiananmen Square?

Pastor ZHANG. Qincheng prison in Beijing.

Chairman SMITH. Okay. I would just note, right after Tiananmen Square, Mr. Wolf and I got into Beijing Prison Number One, where there were 40 activists, all with shaved heads. It looked like a concentration camp, because it was. They were making, as you know, Cochairman Brown, jelly shoes and socks for export to the United States. Under our very ineffective MOU [memorandum of understanding] with China, unless we have real-time information about what's being made by those prisoners, there's no actionable direction that the U.S. Government could take.

We tell them—they, the Chinese—we have suspicions and then they investigate. In this case Mr. Wolf and I walked out with the living proof of what we had gotten ourselves, and I was just wondering if you might have been at that prison because it was horrible. Thin, gaunt men, working around the clock, Reform Through Labor signs all over the place, and their only crime was asking for democracy. So again, I want to thank you and Mr. Li for presenting your very powerful testimony here today.

Chairman Brown?

Senator BROWN. Thank you. I appreciate the discussion of Cisco and some of the comments from Cisco. I know Chairman Smith, and I know Congressman Walz and I, all are troubled by that and we take it seriously. The Commission is looking into its role in the oppression that we see.

Alex, if I can ask you just a brief question. Tell me how your family is doing. Might they suffer from your testimony today? If you would, tell us a little bit about how your family is doing.

Mr. LI. Do you mean now or——

Senator BROWN. Today. Yes, now. Yes.

Mr. LI. I think it will because obviously American—the police—last year I joined a June 4th celebration in San Francisco and the police knew that, and they called my dad to threaten him to warn me not to do anything bad. So I'm pretty sure they know this, and called my dad to threaten.

Senator BROWN. Please let us know. The Commission will monitor any of this. Please let us know if there are any repercussions from your testimony today with your family.

Mr. LI. Sure. Thank you.

Senator BROWN. We want to be on your side and help to protect them as much as we can, as much as you can, together. So, thank you.

Mr. Wu, it's nice to see you again. Thank you for your outspokenness and courage.

Representative WALZ. Well, thank you both. Again, as I said, it's always humbling to sit here and see the folks who are on the front line of fighting for human rights.

Mr. Li, I'm just curious if you can help me. How did your family connect to the Internet? Who is your Internet provider, and how do you do that in China? Who did you pay to have access to? And then your Gmail account you mentioned with your father, how did that work?

Mr. LI. I think it's similar to America. The Internet service was provided by the China Mobile Company.

Representative WALZ. So you had an account. You can get on the Internet. You had a Gmail account.

Mr. LI. Yes. And those Web sites my dad committed on—he was—wanted to overthrow something called Freegate. So those Web sites are blocked in China. That's why he got in trouble.

Representative WALZ. Okay. Well, again, I thank you very much. We've got a panel coming on next that's going to talk about how some of this is done. We're deeply troubled by your account, and

I associate myself with Senator Brown's concern for your family. So, thank you for the courage of coming today, and thank you, Pastor Zhang.

Chairman SMITH. Thank you both. Anything you'd like to add before we go to panel two? We'll be inviting Harry Wu, without objection, to join panel two, a man who has done extraordinary work in exposing the exploitation of the Internet, and especially has brought focus on Cisco. So Harry, if you would just stay there for the second panel, we'd appreciate it.

But would either of you like to add anything before we go to panel two, Mr. Li or Pastor Zhang?

[No response].

Chairman SMITH. Then Harry, we'll go to you in panel two.

Mr. WU. Shall I go?

Chairman SMITH. Yes. Just stay put.

STATEMENT OF HARRY WU, FOUNDER, LAOGAI RESEARCH FOUNDATION AND LAOGAI MUSEUM

Mr. WU. I don't have any connection with any American company that has business with China or the Chinese Government, Chinese companies. I just focus on the Cisco case. There were a number of contracts with China's Security and Public Security Department since 2002 until 2007 or 2008.

China has a national program, the so-called "Golden Shield." Entirely, the whole cost is $5 to $6 billion. So far, I understand that only a few provinces have signed a contract with another American company. Most of them, they signed contracts with Cisco. So we have some quotes here. This is from Chinese information. They so appreciate this cooperation with Cisco, and Cisco has a proposal to them not to only sell the products, sell the equipment, but also to include training.

Last December, I was in Oslo. I wanted to participate in the Nobel Peace Prize award for Chinese dissident Liu Xiaobo. As you know, Liu Xiaobo, since 2002 until 2009, sent 248 articles to our Web site "Guancha," and we published his book.

But unfortunately we saw the Nobel Peace Prize had a menu. On one of the pages, John Chambers, the CEO of Cisco, was there because the CEO supports the Nobel Peace Prize, the financial support for the Nobel Peace Prize awarded to a Chinese dissident. So this is one face to tell the people what Cisco is doing. They sponsor the Nobel Peace Prize awarded to a Chinese dissident, but the other face, they sign a contract—many contracts—for Chinese security to set up the "Golden Shield Program," to arrest Chinese dissidents, including Alex's father, Li Yuanlong and Chen Qiao's father, Liu Xianbin.

You have to know, Liu Xianbin, Chen Qiao's father, was sentenced three times. The first time was two and a half years. The second was 13 years. Recently, this year, he was sentenced to another 10 years in a prison camp. Just because of what? Because he wrote an article on a Web site. How come the Chinese Internet can effectively control everything, control everyone?

I don't think that without Cisco support they could have done it. But we heard Cisco's attorney testify twice in the Senate, in the

House and say, we have to follow Chinese law. We sell the products to anyone. We don't care what they're doing.

But they never mentioned that when they sold the product to Chinese security. They say, "Well, if a car accident happens in a city, the patrol car has to write a report to the supervisor. So, the Internet helps." I say, okay, well, car accident. But if there's a dissident that posts something online, are the police going to report it or not? This is not a security problem, this is a political issue. I want to know that Cisco in China is now training the police.

Let me stop here. I sent a letter to John Chambers, the CEO. I said, "Remember recently IBM apologized to the Jewish because they sold technology to Hitler's Germany 60 years ago. Are you going to apologize later to Chinese dissidents? Because Cisco in this business is entirely working with Chinese Public Security."

Thank you.

Chairman SMITH. Thank you. And let the record note that it was Harry Wu, at the first hearing that I held on Internet exploitation in China, who brought forward the information on Cisco. When we had the Cisco representative, after being sworn in, tell us that they could not disclose what it is that they were doing, and like Google, Yahoo!, and Microsoft, said it was a matter of Chinese law that there was all of this cloak of secrecy.

It was Harry Wu who told us how they had enabled, through Police Net, to give the secret police of China the same capabilities that the FBI, Scotland Yard, and other world-class enforcement agencies have, law enforcement agencies. But we, the United States, and especially through corporations like Cisco, had given them that capability and that capacity.

We will be inviting Cisco back to the witness table and we will ask them hard questions about what it is that they're doing. And as you pointed out so well, Mr. Wu, having spent almost 20 years in the Laogai yourself, and having been tortured beyond belief, without this kind—you know, propaganda and secret police are the two mainstays of dictatorship.

The IBM—and there is a book called IBM and the Holocaust, a heavily footnoted book that makes it very clear that the Gestapo would not have been able to find so many of the Jewish people who ended up at Auschwitz and Buchenwald and elsewhere had it not been for IBM.

Now, fast forward to 2011. Now we have Cisco doing the same kind of horrific enabling of a secret police to track down these great pastors and family members who are behind these lines, going online and then being captured by the secret police because of corporations like Cisco. So, thank you, Mr. Wu, for that. Thank you, Pastor.

Mr. Walz, anything you want to add?

[No response].

Mr. WU. Thank you.

Chairman SMITH. Thank you very much, gentlemen.

We'll now hear from Professor Xiao Qiang. Professor Xiao is an Adjunct Professor at the Graduate School of Journalism at the University of California at Berkeley, and a Visiting Researcher at the Counter-Power Lab at the School of Information at UC-Berkeley as well. Professor Xiao is also Founder and Editor-in-Chief of China

Digital Times, a bilingual Chinese Web site covering China's social and political transition.

We will then hear from Mr. Gil Kaplan, who is partner at King & Spalding, where he focuses on international trade cases and trade policy issues. Mr. Kaplan is also president of the Committee to Support U.S. Trade Laws, an organization of companies, trade associations, unions, and individuals dedicated to preserving and enhancing the trade remedy laws U.S. companies have access to which ensure international trade is conducted on a fair basis.

Professor Xiao?

STATEMENT OF XIAO QIANG, ADJUNCT PROFESSOR, GRADUATE SCHOOL OF JOURNALISM, UNIVERSITY OF CALIFORNIA–BERKELEY; FOUNDER AND EDITOR–IN–CHIEF, CHINA DIGITAL TIMES

Mr. XIAO. Thank you, Mr. Chairman. Respectful Representative Christopher Smith, I have been working with you many years in terms of human rights, promoting human rights in China, and I respect your consistent and tireless work.

I have written a statement to submit to the Commission for the record.

Chairman SMITH. Without objection it will be a part of the record.

Mr. XIAO. So what I'm going to do in the next five minutes will be to briefly summarize a few points to give a background of the Chinese state censorship and the activities on the Chinese Internet of political participation of Chinese netizens and my own analysis and observation in order for us to understand better why there is such censorship and control in the Chinese cyberspace and the consequences to American companies.

First of all, I am currently, in addition to documenting, identifying, and indexing censorship in China, I am also working with some leading computer scientists at UC-Berkeley to test, evaluate, and incubate counter-censorship technologies which can be applied to expand the free flow of information around the world.

The first point I'm going to make on Internet censorship, which is already well documented and publicized in many works, including my own research, is to focus on a single case which is the Chinese Twitter-like company, Sino-Weiboa. China blocked Twitter and Facebook in 2009, but this particular company, who is also raising money from the U.S. stock market, has expanded its own microblogging service in China in the last two or three years. Now it has over 250 million users.

According to their own report, this company has an extensive and powerful censorship mechanism to back up their operation. The company's executive has publicly stated that monitoring the content is Sino-blog services' biggest headache and it entails intensive communication between editors and state managers, including emails, updating guidelines for monitoring content that is sent every hour. This company has hundreds of human hired individuals and departments just to monitor the content and censoring them.

On these particular microblogging services, I have just published the latest directive from the Chinese state censor. Well, actually two of them. One is relating to the artist Ai Weiwei, asking them to delete old information about him borrowing money to return his tax action online. But the latest directive from the state to this company is to prevent three individuals, Chinese individuals, from opening an account on this microblogging service.

These three are Chen Ping, a businessman who is a publisher of a Hong Kong-based magazine called Sunshine Affairs, and the second is called Chang Ping, a renowned Chinese journalist, and third is Wen Yunchao, an editor of that publication. That publication is banned in China and not allowed anywhere in cyberspace, and their names are being prevented from opening any microblogging services in China. These individuals, actually, their personal safety, is in danger.

The next point I'm going to say is that despite this kind of censorship, that the Chinese Internet netizens have been increasing their criticism to the Chinese Government policies and systems and questioning the government accountability and increasing their ability to politically participate in Chinese society.

Precisely because of that, the Chinese Government has intensified its control to a more advanced technological and sophisticated level. And here comes the American companies and technologies, because controlling individuals is not enough. What they are doing is preventing those technologies from search and file sharing, access feeds for blogging, microblogging. They want these Internet services totally under their own control so they don't give foreign companies the same level playing field, and they actually blocked hundreds of thousands, if not more, Web sites and companies and web pages from China, preventing such access for the Chinese netizens.

So it has had both censorship consequences and level trade consequences. My own research group has documented a significant portion of such censorship directives over the last five years, and some are translated on our Web site, and those search-banned key words, over 800 of them, in cyberspace.

So finally my point is, despite such censorship there is an emerging generation of Chinese bloggers and netizens who are pro-human rights, democracy, and freedom values, and actually they are the leading voice on the Chinese Internet. It's the hope of the Chinese Internet to facilitate such speaking voices for a different future of China, but in order to achieve that day, the U.S. Government should stand firmly behind the values of the freedom of speech and freedom of information and do everything we can from this country to mitigate those consequences and violations of human rights and Internet censorship, including this consequence to American companies.

Thank you.

Chairman SMITH. Thank you so very much for your testimony.

Mr. Kaplan?

[The prepared statement of Mr. Xiao appears in the appendix.]

STATEMENT OF GILBERT B. KAPLAN, PARTNER, KING & SPALDING; PRESIDENT, THE COMMITTEE TO SUPPORT U.S. TRADE LAWS

Mr. KAPLAN. Thank you very much, Mr. Chairman and members of the Commission, for inviting me to testify here today. I'd like to just say briefly that I, too, am humbled, as some of you mentioned, to be speaking here with people who have risked their lives, their health, and their families on this issue which we look at perhaps more as a legal and commercial issue, but I understand the deep danger people are in related to this.

Through my work with the First Amendment Coalition, we've been working to achieve a breakthrough on China's Internet restrictions since 2007. I feel that we are finally making some progress, in part from our work and also in part from the work of this commission and other voices on Capitol Hill and the U.S. Trade Representative [USTR].

There is a relationship between commerce and the trade problems we face and American values and our ability to promote American values around the world, and one of those, of course, is free speech.

China's censorship of the Internet and its restrictions on the free flow of information have a very significant impact on U.S. economic and trade interests. These measures have been ongoing for years and have had an overwhelmingly adverse effect on market share for U.S. companies in China, perhaps to the extent that such market share will never be recovered.

China's blocking and filtering measures and the fog of uncertainty surrounding what China's censors will or will not permit violate numerous of China's international obligations, including provisions of the WTO General Agreement on Trade and Services, the GATS.

Although there is public information identifying several large companies that have been blocked or restricted by the Great Firewall, including YouTube, Facebook, Twitter, Vimeo, Google, and The Huffington Post, to name a few, there are many other companies that have been blocked from access in China that I am not able to identify by name specifically because these companies fear retaliation. These companies come from various sectors, including energy, labor mediation, tourism, education, web hosting, and advertising, among others.

The fact that these large, well-established companies and other fast-growing U.S. firms, so successful in every other major market in the world, are reluctant to come forward with specific information that would form the basis of a WTO complaint against the Chinese Government is powerful testament to: (1) the importance of the Chinese Internet market, the largest in the world, to these firms' continuing success; and (2) the risk of retaliation these firms face if they are seen as lending direct support to a trade complaint against China. Moreover, companies not yet in existence but for which China could represent a significant business opportunity do not even have a voice in this matter, and perhaps never will.

The First Amendment Coalition was able to persuade the Office of the U.S. Trade Representative to take the critical step of requesting detailed information from China on its Internet restric-

15

tions under Article 3–4 of the GATS, which mandates transparency in a member's application of measures affecting services.

GATS Article 3–4 reads as follows: "Each member shall promptly respond to all requests by any other member for specific information on any of its measures for general application or international agreements within the meaning of Paragraph 1."

We feel the U.S. request to China under GATS's Article 3–4 is highly significant not only because it is the first time any WTO member has utilized that provision of the GATS agreement, but also because it is the first time that the U.S. Government, or any government, has made a formal submission through the WTO to China to address Internet censorship.

Some of the information requested from China by the USTR included the following: With respect to China's rules governing Web site blocking, who is responsible for determining when a Web site should be blocked? What are the criteria for blocking access? Where are the guidelines published? Who does the actual blocking? How can a service supplier know if their Web site has been blocked? Are decisions to block appealable?

Is the process used to prevent access the same or different for foreign and domestic content? With respect to the prevention of "illegal information," how is illegal information defined? Is a written government order required for a private corporation or relevant authority to block the transmission of illegal information?

We hope, and to some degree expect, that the government of China will answer these questions fully and promptly, fulfilling its obligations under the WTO.

Let me just close by making two points. I think it would be very useful for this Commission to undertake, directly or perhaps through an economic consulting firm, an economic analysis of the overall harm caused to U.S. companies by the Chinese blockage and censorship of the Internet. There isn't really hard economic data on that that's available, but it is a study which could be done. But, of course, someone has to commission it and pay for it. I think that would be a very valuable exercise.

I have talked to economic firms and there is a methodology that could be used. It would be billions of dollars of losses, but I think having that number out there would be very helpful.

Second, in a recent newspaper article a representative of ACT, the Association for Competitive Technology, noted that many of its member companies with joint ventures with firms in China have found their web links back to the United States have been removed or the U.S. firm's Web site has been blocked. He noted, "It's always difficult for technology companies to draw lines in the sand and say this and no further when they are beholden to shareholders." He said, "That's why we need the USTR and the administration to step up to the table."

I concur with this general point. I think we do need government involvement in this and government has to take the lead. Individual companies will not be able to do this without government leadership.

Thank you.

Chairman SMITH. Mr. Kaplan, thank you so very much for your testimony and for laying all of that out for us, and for the work you've done to help get the USTR to take that very important action.

Let me now introduce Mr. Edward Black, who has served as president and CEO of the Computer & Communications Industry Association, a nonprofit membership organization that represents technology companies, including Google, Yahoo!, Ebay, Facebook, and Microsoft. A consistent supporter of Internet freedom, Mr. Black serves on and has previously served as chairman of the State Department's Advisory Committee on International Communications and Information.

Mr. Black, you may proceed.

[The prepared statement of Mr. Kaplan appears in the appendix.]

STATEMENT OF EDWARD BLACK, PRESIDENT AND CEO, COMPUTER & COMMUNICATIONS INDUSTRY ASSOCIATION (CCIA)

Mr. BLACK. Thank you, Chairman Smith, Chairman Brown, and Ranking Member Walz and members of the Commission. I appreciate the opportunity to testify before the Commission to discuss China's censorship of the Internet.

CCIA has promoted openness, competition, and free trade for nearly 40 years and we commend the Commission for examining how restrictions on the free flow of information online pose not only significant human rights concerns, but economic concerns as well.

I know that freedom of expression has mainly been viewed through the lens of human rights. We admire the courage and sacrifice of activists such as Mr. Li's father and Pastor Zhang, who seek freedom for their people and the openness of a free society.

I firmly believe that the United States must continue its fullthroated support of freedom of expression worldwide. We support the State Department's effort to aggressively promote Internet freedom and I caution our government against taking any actions such as misguided intellectual property enforcement bills before Congress that might hamstring these efforts abroad.

In addition to harming human rights, restricting the free flow of information online has serious economic repercussions. American companies whose main purpose is to facilitate communications and information exchange are some of the biggest and fastest-growing companies. Google and Facebook just to mention a few, have estimated market value of $174 and $83 billion respectively. They're both more highly valued than Goldman Sachs. Our industry is an important part of the American economy.

Since China gets full access to U.S. markets in sectors where it has a comparative advantage, it is disconcerting that the U.S. Government has not done more to ensure that our Internet industry gets the same access in China, a market with more Internet users than the entire U.S. population.

However, we are very encouraged by the USTR's recent formal inquiry into the specifics of Chinese censorship. As Gil mentioned, we also had been pushing USTR in this direction for a long time. Using mechanisms available under the WTO, USTR has put China in a position where it needs to divulge specific details about its notoriously vague censorship policy or face repercussions.

The first step of dealing with Chinese restrictions is to bring them into the light of day. Focusing on the impact that such restrictions have on trade provides U.S. negotiators tangible sticks and carrots that are not available in the human rights area. While the WTO allows exceptions to its rules for matters of public morals and national security, it also requires all restrictions be transparent, provide due process, be minimally restrictive, and apply equally to foreign and domestic entities.

As of today, China complies with none of these requirements. Compelling China to justify every blockage may dampen its enthusiasm to impose such measures. We would hope China would have to scale back and better document its censorship practices.

The Chinese Government censors, blocks, and discriminates against foreign-based Web services and content, as discussed more extensively in our written testimony. This directly and indirectly advantages domestic Chinese firms. It has repeatedly blocked sites and services, including Facebook, Flickr, Google, Twitter, and others, singling out U.S. companies for censorship, even when Chinese-owned services carry the same banned content. This double standard strongly suggests that the motivation for censorship is often protectionism rather than morals.

In the past, China has even manipulated the Great Firewall to redirect users entering the URL of U.S. search engines to Baidu. In addition, content filtering by China degrades the quality of service delivered by foreign providers who must compete against unfiltered domestic firms.

Chinese Internet censorship is part of a continuing pattern of using trade and regulatory policies that either restrict access to Chinese markets or force foreign companies to acquiesce to Chinese Government demands as a price of access.

This Commission's most recent annual report correctly identified a troubling aspect of China's censorship regime, where China uses vague standards of liability and places the burden of enforcing those standards on service providers. Pending IP enforcement legislation before this Congress unfortunately shares the same disturbing similarities with China's approach to Internet control, as pointed out by the Commission.

The bills create vague standards for liability and ask private companies and Internet intermediaries to police and censor their users. When coupled with blanket immunity provisions for actions taken while attempting to comply with the legislation, this bill would tolerate and encourage over-broad filtering and will remove legal, as well as illegal, content.

If the United States legitimizes censorship and prior restraints on speech for infringement and enforces it through a draconian system of DNS filtering, this will allow China and others to point to our own actions to justify theirs and make the job of our diplomats very much more difficult.

As a letter from over 100 law professors, including Larry Tribe, recently pointed out, the proposed Protect-IP legislation represents a retreat from the United States' strong support of freedom of expression and the free exchange of ideas on the Internet. We must take care not to undermine our own foreign policy and trade goals by setting bad precedents.

Finally, in conclusion, China's censorship perverts what should be a tool for freedom and empowerment, the Internet, into a tool for authoritarian control. Addressing Chinese censorship as a trade barrier is a legitimate, multilateral, and potentially effective approach that needs to be pursued by our government at the highest levels. It may seem a little bit like going after Al Capone for tax evasion, but that's what we need to do.

Finally, I'd just remind the Commission that I would hope that as the U.S. Government takes action and focuses on this problem, we also keep in mind we want to make sure we do no harm.

Thank you very much.

[The prepared statement of Mr. Black appears in the appendix.]

Chairman SMITH. Thank you very much. I want the record to know that Chairman Brown was called back to the Senate, so he conveys his thanks for your testimony and has told me he has read it and will have some questions that he'll pose for the record.

[The questions appear in the appendix.]

Chairman SMITH. Mr. Walz, I would yield the mike.

Representative WALZ. Well, I thank the Chairman. I, myself, am going to be called away, so the Chairman's compassion and tolerance of me is also appreciated.

So, thank you all for being here. I guess the first question I'm going to ask, maybe each of you—Professor Xiao, this might be to you. I've said this before and I watched it, that everyone said, and I watched with Deng Xiaoping's opening, once the Chinese get television that will change everything. Once the Chinese get land lines that will change everything. Once the Chinese get wireless cell phones that will change everything. We've had this belief that technology would be that overriding social change agent. Is it overly optimistic to believe that this new social media is going to finally be the silver bullet that is unstoppable in terms of their ability to censor?

Mr. XIAO. I don't think anything is a silver bullet. Managing a country is a complicated and huge task, and building democracy and human rights in that society, it's going to be a long, historical process. But technology—and here we're talking about Internet and social media—has some—I'm not a technology deterministic person, but it has an architectural advantages that can—like TV, which is broadcasting an image, the Internet participated and has a networked topology that makes every node have very easy access to post something and information flow much easier.

It's much more difficult for an authoritarian regime to control information, that is true. It's also making the possibility, which never happened before the Internet, for the individuals that can collaborate and coordinate their actions simultaneously or in some kind of self-organized fashion, which any authoritarian regime in China fears the most, is the self-organization of the people.

So these things are actually rapidly happening in the Chinese Internet, in Chinese society, and my research reveals such a pattern, both from language to actual online actions. You mentioned the artist Ai Weiwei, who is right now under the penalty of a $2.4 million tax. It's really political persecution, clearly.

The Chinese censor issued a clear directive to all Internet companies to delete any information regarding the fact that he is using the Internet to collect such loans. Regardless of the censorship and all the effort and all the mechanisms, there are over 30,000 Chinese individuals, with their real names, sending in their little donations. Actually, it's so-called lending money to him as a statement of standing by him, not of the regime. Without Internet, the 30,000 people would not be able to do that. Despite the fact that censorship is, by and large, effective and pervasive.

The Chinese Government is losing their ground to control how much information, particularly their ideology to supporting the regime legitimacy, that they need to be constantly facing contests from the Chinese netizens. So that's actually good news. Despite that, I don't expect this will automatically open the entire society because it has so many other factors to it, but it is positive.

Representative WALZ. No, that is helpful. I think for me, one of the concerns I have is I would anticipate, as you said, that that ability to participate both ways, the ability to self-organize, the things that we're seeing both here and around the world, from Arab Spring to events in the United States. The fear I have is, though, this accelerates further the desire to clamp on it harder will be very tempting.

Mr. XIAO. It is true.

Representative WALZ. And I think we'll see an acceleration in human rights abuses very quickly. So I think now is our time to continue to push before we reach that critical point when they realize they've lost control.

Mr. XIAO. I agree with you.

Representative WALZ. I appreciate that.

I thank both you gentlemen. I appreciate the work you've done. I think that you're approaching this the right way. Mr. Black, I think your suggestion to us is very good to the American public. It's not that they don't care, but I'm a high school teacher so I always look at what motivates people. It's Maslow's hierarchy here. If we're trying to talk about self-actualization on human rights, we're losing them. If you go to the bottom and talk about the money you'll get them, not because they're greedy, but because it impacts them.

Just for an example, is this true? Would this be true in China? I just pulled up Professor Wu's book here, "The Bitter Winds," his memoir, on my Kindle, on my Ipad from Kindle Store, and I want to buy it from Amazon. Could I do that in China? Could I pull up his book in China and buy it? A legitimate business, an American business, a legitimate person who owns that. We couldn't buy this, Mr. Wu?

Mr. WU. My simple answer is no. I don't know about individual books, but many, many books have been blocked.

Mr. BLACK. Your point is well taken.

Representative WALZ. Amazon is losing money today.

Mr. BLACK. There are a lot of things in the United States that would be blocked for a variety of reasons, commercial activity and products galore are basically not allowed.

Representative WALZ. If you're a free market capitalist here, this has to really appall you, doesn't it?

Mr. BLACK. Absolutely.

Representative WALZ. Here's an entrepreneur that did this, put this on there. He and the company, Amazon, who are benefiting from it, the content, would be stopped from doing that.

Mr. BLACK. There are studies that indicate that Internet commerce over the past year has basically amounted to $2 trillion worth of activity. A substantial amount of that was not in China. You could imagine how much—when a Web site is blocked, all the advertisers, all the products that might flow through that lose that channel. So the impact is not on the Web site itself only, it is on a wide range of players that interact with that in a variety of ways.

Representative WALZ. There's a ripple effect on jobs here. Today there's going to be a worker not needed to box this book, there's going to be a worker not needed to load it on a UPS or FedEx truck to send it to this person who would liked to have ordered it and couldn't.

Mr. KAPLAN. That's correct. Even more problematic, Amazon does function in China but it has had to do a joint venture with a Chinese company and have servers set up within China. So one of the macro effects of the whole censorship is many U.S. companies have had to move to China, can't use their facilities in the United States, and this has a very pervasive effect on U.S. economic prosperity.

Representative WALZ. That's a powerful point.

I'm sorry I'm going to have to leave, Mr. Chairman, but I look forward to hearing the rest of this. I do want to convey how much I thank you on this, and I certainly think you are hitting on a powerful tool here that can have multiple benefits, both from human rights and economic fairness. So, I thank you for that.

Chairman SMITH. Thank you.

Representative WALZ. Mr. Chairman, thank you for letting me go.

Chairman SMITH. Thank you, Mr. Walz. I want to thank our very distinguished witnesses for your insights and counsel.

Just a couple of questions. Professor Xiao, has the capacity to censor and survey within China been developed primarily by U.S. IT companies and U.S. corporations, or Western corporations? If that is the case, is it still the case—or was the case—today or has the technology of the Chinese, Baidu and the others in the government, collaboration with them, caught up and now they've taken it over? They basically can do it on their own without——

Mr. XIAO. At the beginning, early stage of the Internet development, it's clearly the case that those technologies are almost directly imported from the United States. In the last 10 years, however, China has sort of emphasized to develop such technology capacity by its own companies or own trusted engineers. However, those Chinese Government-trusted domestic companies, many of them have close relationships with U.S. companies. There is a technology transfer clearly happening in sort of a second or third tier to the Chinese censorship apparatus.

Chairman SMITH. Let me ask, Mr. Kaplan, Mr. Black, has there been any effort made by the Department of Defense, Commerce, and all of the relevant agencies of the U.S. Government to ensure that this technology is not conveyed to the Chinese secret police and the military? Obviously the dual use for the military cannot be underscored enough. Command and control is essential to an effective operating military machine.

When you give it to police who routinely torture people who go on the Net and try to promote fundamental democratic values, it seems to me we should be inhibiting the sale and transfer of that capability. Has that happened at all during either the Bush administration, the Clinton administration before it, or now the Obama administration?

Mr. BLACK. Yes. Basically it's an export control issue which goes back for decades to the Soviet Union, et cetera. The rules have kind of evolved, but historically were to differentiate between those things where getting the product had a tremendous difference, and whether or not there was foreign availability, either domestic or from a third party, third country.

Generally, although there are certain things that are clearly so obnoxious and repulsive that they remain on what we call foreign policy controls and banned, to a large extent I think there was a broad spectrum of agreement that when something is widely available in an indigenous way as well, that it is just futile to really have those controls.

Again, carving out some really horrendous things, but one of the great examples we went through was with semiconductors. Semiconductors clearly were important to the creation in the East bloc of sophisticated computers for weapons control, but they were also used for transistor radio and everything else. So they were so widely available from so many sources, so we just can't control it, so we focused on the things we can really make a difference with. That's pretty much a prevailing U.S. law. So there's not a real effort because they don't think it would have an impact.

The question, do you judge it by, will it make a difference at the end of the day? The second standard is, even if it will make a difference, is it so abhorrent that you don't want to be connected to it? Those two standards coexist and apply in different ways.

Chairman SMITH. Well, with respect, as far as you can tell, was there any instance where the government said that's not going to be sent over to the PRC because we know it has consequences for the dissidents and the religious believers who go online and are seeking to——

Mr. BLACK. In the software world, I'm not sure. There's clearly a more physical product category. There are those, a number of things in that category, but I'm not sure I'm aware of any in the software.

Mr. KAPLAN. Frankly, I'm not sure. But I would like to make a related point. The irony about all this in terms of China, is we've allowed the entire manufacturing base, as it relates to the Internet, to be put in China. Knowing the products that you need to run the Internet aren't really made in the United States anymore, or are made to a very limited degree, it always was the deal that, sort of at the higher end, more intellectual capital would stay in the United States and we'd sell that to China. That's like what we're trying to sell over the Internet.

So we've moved all the hardware to China so they obviously can build off that to control the Internet because all the hardware is made there. We don't make it, but we were supposed to be able to sell the higher end stuff, like Internet, R&D, and other things like that to China, and now they're stopping our Internet. So, the whole deal is, you know, our Internet providers, our Internet—exciting opportunities like Facebook, Twitter, and other organizations could be very profitable and bring more prosperity here. So the whole deal is askew very fundamentally.

Chairman SMITH. Point well taken. And that continues to this day?

Mr. KAPLAN. It gets worse every day.

Chairman SMITH. It gets worse.

Mr. XIAO. It's getting worse.

Chairman SMITH. Doesn't that strike you as absurd that the West—I mean, even the idea of foreign availability being a loophole, I mean, Semens, a lot of companies, corporations that have tremendous capabilities, but the Chinese wanted what Google, what Cisco, what others could provide because it was at least——

Mr. XIAO. Let me emphasize this point. The aspects of the Internet innovation, particularly other users and moving the content that will make them more easily accessible, more easy to organize, more easy for users to use the nature of those Internet innovations, but those Internet innovations directly run against the Chinese Government interest to control information from the top down. It's not those companies trying to run against China, this is Internet innovation. The Chinese companies try to do the same innovation, but they cannot do it in China.

So it hurts the innovation in Chinese society as well. Censorship hurts both countries. But also, because the Chinese Government feels they cannot control such a new innovation, therefore, especially the empowering users aspect of those innovations, therefore, they block the foreign companies for which they think they don't have direct control and they put all kinds of demands and shackles on the domestic companies to make the domestic Internet industries also handicapped in that aspect.

Mr. BLACK. If I could add?

Chairman SMITH. Yes, please.

Mr. BLACK. No doubt that China has developed tremendous technological capability. That's absolutely true. The United States is still a leader in Internet innovations in terms of how to utilize in creative and imaginative ways the Internet because we care about empowerment. Basically what the Internet does in many ways is it empowers users. That empowerment allows those users to feed back in a social network way to help be part of the innovation process.

So the U.S. society, not just our companies, is really the dynamic, creative component trying to relax from ever being able to do that because they're not letting their people have that empowerment. They fear the empowerment. So there's always going to be some lag there, and frankly, our social networks are—if you think in First Amendment terms, it's not just freedom of speech, it's freedom of association. It is a tremendously useful tool.

The fact that China so fears some of those companies having a presence there because of the openness of our companies' systems, therefore they create their parallels and their alternatives and put much more, greater restrictions on it. So they recognize the power of the Internet and they are trying to use the benefits of it, and yet trying very hard to restrict aspects of it which they feel they can't control.

Chairman SMITH. In your view—all three of your views—my sense is that China is becoming much more xenophobic than ever, that the dictatorship believes that the restlessness, especially the thought of a Jasmine Revolution in what they were seeing in the Middle East, sent shivers down their spine, especially when there was some crackling over the Internet about freedom and democracy. Those things began to percolate again. Not that they ever went away, but they were more suppressed. I've held 34 hearings on human rights abuses in China.

Several of those hearings have focused on the grossly destabilizing consequences of the one-child-per-couple policy, forced abortion, the missing girls. The State Department said 10 years ago, the State Department reports there may be as many as 100 million missing girls in China—that was 10 years ago—through sex-selection abortions and gendercide.

I work on trafficking, human trafficking all the time. China is becoming a magnet beyond any other comparison for trafficking women and girls. The woman who wrote the book, Bare Branches recently testified and said that by 2020, 40 to 50 million men—so the number has one up in terms of estimation—will not be able to find wives because they have been killed systematically through the one-child-per-couple policy.

The point being, the government now looks at this growing instability, more males than females by far, a growing lawlessness. It seems there's a total direct relationship between that and a tightening of just—the Wall Street Journal, on November 6, said, "Executives from China's top Internet companies pledged to boost efforts to curb harmful content at a unusual government meeting with web firms." It goes on to say that "Baidu, Alibaba, and Sina Corp have said that Internet companies must strengthen their self-management, self-restraint, and strict self-discipline." We all know what those words mean. They're just tightening that iron fist.

I'm wondering, the instability is going to reach a tipping point. I'm deeply worried about what that means for more torture, as you are, I'm sure, more killings in the streets, as we've seen. I mean, Tiananmen Square was the most visible, but there have been others since, as we all know. That connection, if you will——

Mr. XIAO. Let me share some of my research and observations on this. One, is my research group has documented over 3,000 blocked URLs by the Great Firewall. This is far from the entire number of them, but these are the Web sites submitted by Chinese netizens. So, to some degree it's they are useful for them directly, so you can see the pattern of where they are blocking not only just politically-sensitive information, but any sort of user-generated contents that a hosting service feels they cannot control.

The second is that the directives, we have documented over the last five years, as I said, a significant body, a proportion of it. You can analyze a pattern of it. The increasing xenophobia is correct by how many directives goes after the so-called massive incidents, basically corrective actions at the local level protests in China is increasing. So the control of such information flow online has been increasing in the last five years, clearly.

Also, you can look at the sensitive words that they ban or block, a Sino-blog or a microblog service. They ban the search because then the user cannot find all the related information. They are afraid of such an information aggregation phenomenon in the Chinese Internet. So we documented over 820 such words, which is only a portion of it, but it's already clearly showing what kind of fear that they have of the site. Again, there's a pattern and there's a trend to increasing state instability.

Finally, regarding the family planning policy, I have a clear example between the Internet and that, which is, as you've probably heard, about a Chinese lawyer, Chen Guangcheng, the blind man who helped villagers in his village and neighborhood to defend their rights, including the one-child policy and abusive practices and forced abortion, et cetera.

He's been sentenced and now he's been released. He served his sentence already and he's supposedly free, but he's not free at all. He lives in the village and is incommunicado. Nobody can visit so no one knows what's happened to him. So on the Chinese Internet, the netizens started this movement of, just go to visit him.

Those villagers are being blocked, beaten, harassed, and tortured and sent away from the village by the local authorities. The central authority clearly knows what's going on and those activities are also banned on the Chinese Internet, but the Chinese netizens are privately organizing anyway. So it's an ongoing case at this moment, linked between the government's fear to some of the policies and challenges and the ability of mobilization on the Internet.

Chairman SMITH. Yes?

Mr. BLACK. If I could, I think your question basically is, yes, we sense a greater assertiveness, boldness, unashamedness about, and really defending their approach about how to censor the Internet, not backing away at all. In fact, I think they realize that there is a global contest going on, whether or not an open model would prevail or a closed model, and they're competing, I think, to get the rest of the world to adopt their model, partly because I think they believe in it and partly because it prevents them from becoming an outlier.

The more people they can persuade into being a censorship type country, the more they can say, well, we're doing what everybody does. I think that's a key part of what's driving them. I think it's important to understand the newest tactic that they're really using. It's not that new, but in many cases it's not the government doing the censorship, it is imposing liability on Internet intermediaries and thereby compelling them, forcing them, encouraging them very strongly to be their self-censors. That's the model.

I think the model that they're actually going to sell around the world is not that the governments do it themselves, because most governments don't have the technological capability. It will be to create this model of imposed liability, economic liability that would put people out of business if they don't become effective censors.

Mr. KAPLAN. Maybe I could just add, as the United States loses more and more ground in the trade battles, I think with China, China has become much more assertive and brazen in terms of promoting its values within China, but within the rest of the world, too. I'm sure you've looked at the situation in Africa, Latin America, the relationship to the World Bank and how they're competing with them in terms of loans. If we keep losing economic power we're going to lose moral power over values.

This relates to the question that Congressman Walz asked. I think China is going to be very successful in controlling the Internet. It will not open up Chinese society because they have such a pervasive ability and such a pervasive desire to do it. They will be able to do it. They can defeat the positive sides of the Internet. There's been press in totalitarian societies forever, but the press has not meant freedom of the press. There's not going to be freedom of the Internet in China, I don't think. But they are being successful in controlling the Internet, essentially, unless this commission and other people can do something about it.

Mr. XIAO. If I could add one more point, which is demanding transparency, why it's important. Clearly it's important to demand transparency in how they censor the Internet because the business is imperative to have such a level playing field. It also has very positive consequences for human rights, expanding human rights in Chinese society, because the whole censorship is about controlling people's minds.

The most effective censorship is not letting people know what's being censored and what's being controlled. The more what is being censored and what exists in the censorship itself is known more clearly in detail by many people, the less effective that censorship is and the more people will demand more human rights and freedom of speech in Chinese society.

Chairman SMITH. You know, Professor Xiao, last week members of our Commission staff and myself sought the ability to go to meet with Chen Guangcheng and his wife, Yuan, and were denied a visa. We are repeating that request to the Chinese Embassy in the hope that we would be able to. I believe it was his 40th birthday on Saturday.

We wanted to be there with him and his wife and show solidarity, and hopefully to let the Chinese know that we are watching and the world is watching, because our great fear is that they will beat him, and beat him to death, which they've been doing since he was in prison and since he's been released. So, thank you for bringing that up, because that's so very important.

Let me ask about—and I only have two final questions to this excellent panel. In 2006, I introduced the Global Online Freedom Act. I am going to reintroduce it very shortly. The idea, and we're working on text to see what might be the best way of accomplishing what I know we all agree to, but obviously means to that end are sometimes open to debate—always open to debate.

But the idea would be to establish an Internet-restricting country designation, because obviously China is not the only country in the world where this is a problem. I just chaired a hearing on Belarus yesterday, or two days ago. Belarus, with President Lukashenko remains one of the worst dictatorships—is the last dictatorship—to do it, and they use Internet censoring, courtesy of the Chinese model, with great impunity and obviously capture a lot of dissidents and democracy activists.

So they would be surely designated an Internet-restricting country and would require disclosure of what is being censored, whether it be Microsoft, Google, or any of the others. It would require that personally identifiable information be put out of reach of the Chinese or any other Internet police.

To their credit, Yahoo! made a move when they went to Vietnam to put that information out of reach, and it's in another ASEAN [Association of Southeast Asian Nations] country, I'm happy to say, because there was instance after instance where Internet bloggers and the like were put into prison simply for expressing concerns about the dictatorship in that country. That's one approach.

The other approach, and I would appreciate your views on this as well if you would, the Falun Gong practitioners and some of their IT experts have developed a capability that I have spent hours, and as I said, Frank Wolf and others, trying to understand because it is above my pay grade in terms of technological understanding, but they seem to have a means of piercing the Great China firewall, and to do so almost at will, if not at will.

We've asked the administration repeatedly to honor the appropriations amount that was set aside by Mr. Wolf on the Appropriations Committee to take this and run with it and to fund it so that this firewall is not impenetrable, and they have shown that, and it can also be used in other Internet-restricting countries as well. So your take on the Falun Gong's technology, GOFA [Global Online Freedom Act], those two things.

Mr. XIAO. Okay. Since my research lab has done a lot of focus on this area, let me just say some general points. One, is that the Great Firewall is far from watertight. It actually has thousands of leaks all the time. They are doing a quite incredible job in terms of preventing information from reaching the scale of the masses, millions of certain information, but also they have not been doing it in their full capacity because I don't think they're better resources, but their sort of policy decision about what time, it's not a time of crisis to do such more intensive blocking at this moment, but it's cranking up all the time.

There's probably four types of technology and practices that are sort of leaking the otherwise blocked information into the Chinese cyberspace. The one type of practice is mostly set up by Chinese techies themselves using the U.S. servers or servers outside of the Great Firewall and set up some circumvention tunnels. So if you know a little bit of technology, it's not hard to do it by yourself, to share it with your friends.

Those activities are small enough that the Great Firewall will never find out all of them. There's just too many of them. Those practices have been shared, the knowledge is being shared, and the total number doing that actually in Chinese cyberspace is very significant, I would say a significant portion of the entire sort of information flow that way.

The second significant portion of people doing that is by VPN, the commercial tunneling technology, because the company needs that, or many services need that. People just pay by the service and then you can circumvent the Great Firewall, but you have to pay the money for it. A lot of people for a variety of needs, not only political needs, business and other things, have to do that. The

Great Firewall can block them, but because they are afraid of consequences and collateral damage, they're not doing so at this moment most of the time.

Third, are those circumvention tools, including the Falun Gong group's introduced and managed tools. It has been, in a variety of situations, very effective for the other users, particularly that are user-friendly, when they are user-friendly and simple to download or simple to use. They're not limited to Falun Gong tools. There's other tools out there. But they all have different strengths and weaknesses.

None of them can be absolutely blocked by the Great Firewall at all, but there's a battle of cat-and-mouse going at it all the time. So this side of the research and development and deployment of circumvention tools does need to be supported and expanded and helped by the information flow. So, all of these activities are important.

Mr. KAPLAN. The issues that were just discussed, certainly that's my understanding also. There are means to get past the firewall, but as soon as they become generally known I think the Chinese will find ways to patch those holes and then other means will be found. But it is not airtight, by any means. There are people who have gotten through in any number of ways, so I think that can be done.

But it's a cat-and-mouse game: You do one thing, they'll do another; you do another, and it slows down the ability to get information in China. I mean, if you talk to U.S. students or U.S. citizens in China, most of them have given up trying to use U.S. Web sites. It just takes so long and it's so undependable. So you don't have to stop it entirely to make it essentially not useful.

Mr. XIAO. Right. I'll give you an example. The Google Gmail server, the Gchat, and the Chinese Government, since the spring, has disconnected that connection to the Gchat every 10 minutes or every 15 minutes. So that type of thing is annoying enough for a lot of people to stop using those services and that's what they're doing. They don't completely cut it off, but they'll create such a burden that it forces the users to use other Chinese services.

Mr. BLACK. I might use a metaphor to make the same point that has been made, which is, if you don't think of it as the wall, think of it as a dam and the fertilizer for freedom and it'll trickle out. They're never going to have a 100 percent sure way that nothing has penetrated. But the trouble is, it's really successfully blocking the valley below from being fertilized with the full knowledge of the Internet and that's sad.

Chairman SMITH. Mr. Kaplan, if I could ask you, and all of you if you want to answer, prior to China's ascension into the WTO and PNTR, I held a series of hearings in my Subcommittee on Human Rights about why we were so naive to think that China would adhere to the rules and regulations prescribed by the WTO, since they did not live up to virtually any of the human rights commitments that they had made, including the Universal Declaration of Human Rights.

As we all know, they have so deigned the International Covenant for Civil and Political Rights, which they violate with impunity. For at least a half a dozen years before any Chinese official came to the United States, they would announce that they were close to signing it to try to mitigate any kind of criticism that official would receive here. Totally gamed it. After a while, you say, how many times are we going to get hit and say, oh, they didn't really mean it?

Now, you have brought out, Mr. Kaplan, in great detail, and I join in what you helped to bring about and I thank you for that, but under WTO the rules have been broken. At least, we believe they are, and I think they are. What can the WTO—where's the enforcement, because that's what always seems to be lacking? A slap on the wrist. At what point is there a genuine, durable penalty for violating, in this case, the trade laws?

Mr. KAPLAN. Well, I think there are two answers to that question. One, is I think there's an awful lot the United States could be doing to impose consequences on China for the violation of our trade rights. We could be self-initiating many more cases, we could take some of the emergency powers that are available to impose tariffs on products coming into the United States.

We could start acting much more vigorously on currency. We're doing, I would say, a very small percentage of what we could do to pressure China to comply with their international trade obligations, putting aside the WTO, and we ought to be doing a lot more than we're doing in that regard.

I hope at some point we do turn up the heat, because I think it will have consequences if our actions have direct consequences on Chinese imports to the United States of major high value items, I think we've got to start doing that.

As to the WTO, if they do not answer these questions that USTR has asked fully and honestly we can start a WTO case. Now, that's litigation, it takes a while. But the WTO has shown itself willing to impose decisions on everybody, including the Chinese, if they close their market unfairly. This is a market-closing device they're using. If they don't comply, we can retaliate.

We can put duties on their computers coming into the United States. We can put duties on other products coming into the United States. It might be appropriate to pinpoint Internet-related technologies. We are able to do that. Usually when that happens, foreign governments, even very big and strong ones, do change their conduct.

Mr. BLACK. One thing I think is not fully understood is, again, I think there's a great way to bring pressure on China by focusing on the rest of the world as well. There are difficulties in bringing China cases, but we should bring them. I totally agree that's there. But there are other countries doing similar things. It may be much easier to establish a string of precedents against some countries without the capability, frankly, to push back both politically, diplomatically, and legally.

Setting a string of WTO precedents in this area might be very helpful. Since, again, my focus is Internet freedom in general, although China has to be a big part of that discussion, I would step out of focus here and mention that right now Russia is in the process of seeking WTO admission. Because of the U.S. Jackson-Vanik legislation there is a unique lever.

I am not aware of what confirmed enforceable commitments in the area of Internet freedom are being requested of Russia, but I would certainly think it would be within the framework of anybody who cares about these issues to try to make that so, and again that would then be a fantastic precedent to deal with China.

Chairman SMITH. Is there anything else any of you would like to add before we close?

Mr. BLACK. If I could make one short——

Chairman SMITH. Mr. Black?

Mr. BLACK [continuing].—sentence I didn't get to read. Our Nation invented the Internet. We invented a First Amendment. We're the global standard-bearer for both economic and political freedom. It's critical that we continue as a country to lead in holding Chinese and other governments accountable. Part of that is, we also do have to remember, you must lead by example as well as by word. Thank you.

Chairman SMITH. If I could ask—I should have ended on that, but would any of you like to make a comment on Cisco and their enabling of the Police Net and other means by which they enable the secret police?

Mr. XIAO. I'm sorry. I actually would rather echo what was just said about, America invented the Internet and the First Amendment. I grew up in China, but became a U.S. citizen five years ago. When I swore into this country's citizenship, I was deeply, profoundly moved by the diversity of the people to unite in the same house on fundamental human rights and dignity. But I am always Chinese in a sense of cultural heritage, and for my work am deeply connected with the people in China. Particularly, I became an activist since the 1989 Tiananmen massacre.

I actually know for a fact that when the Internet was introduced to China in the middle 1990s, many of the enthusiastic people, entrepreneurs, and technologists and the Internet industry with the hope that they are the Tiananmen generation. Our dream of China's democracy has been crushed by tanks in 1989, but they're the same people that have hope that this time technology will be on our side and we will change China.

There are so many Internet entrepreneurs and the business people and content providers that I know that share that dream. Even though they are working under the censorship, and some of them are working inside of the system, but that dream never died. So the freedom of the Internet is not only an American dream, but it's also a new Chinese dream that has not been flourishing. I still continue working toward that.

Mr. KAPLAN. I think that was a very moving statement. I would just add, I really think the United States has to be prepared to take action in terms of real economic consequences. I think if we did do that more frequently it would make an enormous difference and I hope we will be more willing to do that in the future.

Chairman SMITH. Thank you so very much for your testimony, for your leadership, and those very uplifting and encouraging notes, but also challenging notes.

The hearing is adjourned.

Mr. LI. I have one last comment.

Chairman SMITH. Okay. We'll reopen for a moment to hear Mr. Li.

Mr. LI. This is pretty short. I am sitting here today because I have the hope that more people will come over in the future, so I wish those companies have some confessions on those who suffered and those victims here.

Chairman SMITH. I would agree. We had a hearing with Shi Tao's mother a few years back, and Jerry Yang sat right behind where Shi Tao was. At the time there was an ongoing lawsuit against Yahoo!. Frankly, Jerry Yang seemed to have been truly moved by the plight of Shi Tao in particular, and his mother's agony as she talked about her son still to this day in prison, but obviously then having gotten a 10-year sentence.

I asked him if he would settle that lawsuit and help the individuals who were—the families, as we all know, get impoverished while a loved one goes off to the laogai, and Harry Wu has been working very closely with them and others to make sure that the families are helped. So there is a conscience, I think, in corporate America. I think it needs to be prodded sometimes. I do believe that Google thought at first that they were opening China rather than contributing to its further closure.

But as Professor Xiao pointed out, almost like judo, no matter how hard the secret police hits you can still throw them if you have the skill and the technological acumen. But there is that sense that an apology or tangible help, and to realize that you can't enable a dictatorship. I would conclude my comments, that I believe dictatorships need two things to survive: The control of the message, the propaganda message, and secret police.

In Cisco, they're getting both, especially the secret police enabling, but I think many—I mean, Google actually supports the Global Online Freedom Act. At first, they were vigorously opposed to it. Again, no legislation is panacea or a silver bullet ever, but it may be a useful tool if we can get it enacted. So, thank you for that very important note.

Mr. Black, did you want to—you leaned forward like you wanted to join in.

Mr. BLACK. I wanted to add, when you mentioned Falun Gong, the kind of circumvention tools that it uses are in fact one of the things that makes us concerned about this intellectual property protection legislation, SOPA [Stop Online Piracy Act]. Those kind of tools would probably be made illegal. So again, lead by example is a big issue. I guess I'd also maybe use this occasion to mention that we have just begun and have created a new foundation to ensure Internet freedom for an innovative future. It's the Foundation for Innovation and Internet Freedom. We believe that there needs to be another voice that can work globally for this, again, focusing on innovation, the economic component, as well as Internet freedom itself. So we're in this fight for a long time.

Chairman SMITH. Thank you. And thank you all for your testimony.

The hearing is adjourned.

[Whereupon, at 11:51 a.m. the hearing was concluded.]

APPENDIX

PREPARED STATEMENTS

PREPARED STATEMENT OF ALEX LI

NOVEMBER 17, 2011

My name is Muzi Li (or Alex). I am from Bijie City, Guizhou Province, China. My father is Yuanlong Li, a man who was sent to jail for two years for publishing four articles online. I came to the United States on December 28, 2009 and became an undergraduate student at Bowling Green State University. I am majoring in Economics and minoring in Philosophy. Due to my fear of the Chinese Government's Ministry of State Security, I applied for political asylum in the United States in December 2010. I was approved on March 8, 2011.

My family bought a computer when I was in middle school. My father didn't know how to use a computer, so I taught him. He learned some basic skills, such as how to use the Internet. However, my father and I found that we could Google some websites, but we could not visit them because those websites' opinions differed from the Chinese government's. At the beginning of 2005, I got Freegate from a friend. Freegate is proxy software; through Freegate, I could cross the firewall to visit foreign websites with different ideas. Later on, my father published his articles overseas through Freegate's software.

Unfortunately, those four articles became my family's nightmare. The nightmare lasted for two years and five days. On the morning of September 9, 2009, my stepmother called me and told me not to come home until that afternoon. In the afternoon, I went back home and saw that the computer was missing and my house had been searched. My stepmother was weeping. Then I found out my father was arrested that day at his working place by the agents from the Ministry of State Security without any notice. Meanwhile, another group of agents visited my stepmother at her work place. They drove her home and rummaged through my home in front of her. She told me not to go home in the morning because she did not want me to be scared.

Later the agents found out that I taught my father how to operate the computer; they decided to interrogate me. I was 17 in 2005, not yet an adult. They took me to a hotel to interrogate me without my parents' permission; they did not allow my mother or my stepmother to stay with me during the interrogation. During the interrogation, the agents tried to prove that I was an accomplice of my father. They asked me some questions such as, "How much do you know about your father's articles?" "Did you help your father write the articles?" They told me that my father had already told them what he did. They wanted me to tell them what I knew. If our stories matched, my father would be safe, and nothing would happen to him. In that case, I told them that I taught my father how to use the computer, and how I got the Freegate software. The agents lied; they threw my father to the jail then.

A few weeks later, the agents came to my home. They asked me a confusing question: "How did your father publish those articles? Did he use your email address?" I explained that everyone knows to publish an article on a forum website, instead of using email, all you need to do is copy and paste. Besides, my father had a Yahoo! email account, so he didn't even know my Hotmail password. How could he have used my email address to publish articles on a forum? Thus, I told the police officers it was impossible for him to have used my email address. The reason why the agents could see my *omegacepearee@hotmail.com* email address was because I used it to register for our family's Windows software. So, when the agents found my IP address, they found the email address for the operating system, and assumed it was what my father used to post the articles.

Nevertheless, the agents heard what they wanted, and ignored the rest. They ignored my answer about the email address. They also adopted my words during the first interrogation as part of their evidence.

The reasoning behind the sentencing was that my father published four articles, which were viewed 1,532 times and received responses from over 25 people. The court stated my father was guilty of "inciting subversion of state power and overthrowing the socialist system." First of all, my father posted his articles on foreign-operated websites. Without a proxy, people in China could not visit them. In 2005, few people knew of and made use of proxy software. Secondly, I could not imagine a nation with 1.4 billion people would be overthrown by an article with 1,532 views and responses from 25 people. So, I believe the agents were just using this as an excuse to persecute my father.

Moreover, I suspect China's judicial system. While my father was detained, the Ministry of Police and State Security, the Court and the Procurator spoke with one voice; they all thought my father sinned by publishing four articles. They threatened me saying that if I talked of my father's case to overseas media, the penalty for my father would be even more serious.

This is the disparaging situation and terrifying government that I faced while in China. Finally, my father advised me to leave the country. He sacrificed by selling his house to pay my tuition in the United States. He repaid the house mortgage with the help of the Yahoo! Foundation, and then he sold it. In the United States, I took part in some activities like the memorial event for Tiananmen Square. The agents in China knew exactly when and where I was and what I did at these activities.

I do not believe the agents could get this detailed information without collaborating with an information technology company of the likes of Cisco Systems, who has built China's Golden Shield from the ground up.

This is my testimony.

Pastor John Zhang's Testimony

Ladies and Gentlemen:

Hello, my name is Qianjin Zhang. I am currently serving as the pastor of the Bay Area Reformed Evangelical Church in San Francisco.

22 years ago, in 1989, I was a Language and Literature student at Beijing Language and Culture University. I actively participated in the 1989 Patriotic Democratic Movement in Beijing.

After the Tiananmen Square Incident, I organized a large memorial service to remember the people who were massacred at Tiananmen. I was arrested on June 15th on charges of "instigating counterrevolutionary propaganda" and sent to Beijing's Qincheng Prison for two years.

After being released, I was expelled from Beijing and went to Hainan, where I had to fend for myself.

In 2001, I was baptized as a Christian; it was not long after that that I became a leader in an underground house church. Every Sunday I would lead dozens of Christians in worship in hotels, restaurants or in followers' homes. Then, on the night before the 15th anniversary of the Tiananmen Square Incident, I was illegally detained for 10 days.

I came to the U.S. in 2006 to study Theology. Graduating in 2009 with a Masters in Biblical Studies, I found a position with a church in the San Francisco Bay Area.

While I was in Seminary, I would visit the Goddess of Democracy statue in San Francisco every year on the anniversary of the Tiananmen Square Incident. I would also actively participate in sending Christmas and New Year's greeting cards to prisoners of conscience in China. This was a good reminder to all Chinese immigrants, currently living in this free country, not to forget the blood and sweat of those who sacrificed their lives by the millions fighting for democracy in China.

While I was in China, my entire family suffered under China's persecution and everyday we lived in fear and without freedom. When Zhao Ziyang passed away, the police placed my family under house arrest for a month. We would have a police car "escort" us everywhere we went. Even when my daughter went to her piano proficiency exam, the police drove a police car to send her to the testing site. After arriving in America, while I was enjoying prosperity and democracy, I would, think about all the dissidents being persecuted in China. I teamed up with colleagues in the Bay Area to participate in Chinese humanitarian relief efforts. We would raise funds annually to provide humanitarian support and aid to victims of unjust treatment in China due to social, political and/or religious reasons. We also call them often to comfort and encourage them. Starting in 2007 up until today, annually, we support over one hundred victims and their families.

In 2009 we helped Fang Zheng, a man whose legs were crushed by a tank during the Tiananmen Square Incident, and his family escape from China and relocate to the U.S. In

Pastor John Zhang's Testimony

2010, we helped raise funds for Li Muzi, son of Guizhou Democracy Party member Li Yuanlong, to come to the U.S. and helped him gain legal residence so that he could graduate. Using Microsoft's Hotmail, Li Yuanlong wrote "Becoming American, in Ideology," plus three other articles under the pseudonym "Night Wolf" and posted them on foreign websites. For this he was charged with "inciting subversion of state power."

Liu Xianbin, a dissident from Sichuan, posted three articles online calling for the Communist Party to implement political change. For this Liu was sentenced on March 25, 2011 by the Sichuan Suining City's Intermediate Court to 10 years in prison for "inciting subversion of state power." This is Liu's third stint in prison. He is 43 years old and has celebrated 11 birthdays in the darkness of his prison cell. When his daughter, Chen Qiao, was only two years old, Liu was taken from her life. When she was eight or nine, during her winter vacations, she and her mother would take the train to Nanchong, and from there take the bus to Dazhu- a trek that would take up a whole day- to go visit her father in prison. Chen's interactions with her father were limited to letters and sketches sent out at intervals predetermined by the prison. Thus Chen's memory of her father is fuzzy and distant. When she was 11 years old in 2009, her father suddenly appeared at their home. He was like a stranger intruding into her calm life. Feeling guilty about his absence, Liu wanted to spend more time with his wife and daughter. However, on March 25, 2011, the Communist Party sentenced Liu to yet another stint in prison, where he will waste away for the next 10 years. Chen Qiao is now 14. She and her father have spent less than four years together. A girl's adolescent years are when she needs her father most. She will not have the opportunity to get spoiled by her father or horse around with him, nor can she receive her father's love, guidance or protection.

The American company Cisco has played a disgraceful role in Liu Xianbin's sad story. According to reports, Cisco knowingly helped China's Ministry of Public Security construct the "Golden Shield Project" as well as provided equipment, technology and training. The "Golden Shield Project" is a national surveillance network system that has a huge database and a sophisticated tracking network system. Thanks to network surveillance technologies provided by Cisco, the Ministry of Public Security can trace dissidents' IP addresses and then track, harass and arrest them. I saw this in four articles published on Cisco's Chinese website, clearly showing the cooperative relationship between Cisco and China's Ministry of Public Security. Without a doubt, Cisco is responsible for the deterioration of internet freedom in China. I hope that the Commission will enter these documents into the record.

Today, I want to remind everyone that freedom of speech is an inherent right given to man by God; it is an inalienable right. The U.S. was established on Christian values. The U.S. should defend and adhere to these universal human values and promote "non-evil" business practices. Each member of Congress has the responsibility to monitor American companies like Cisco, who are trying to maximize business interests in China. These companies should not ignore the most basic morals and principles of business ethics. In order to regulate the business practices of companies that violate American law, they should be subject to public criticism, condemnation, economic penalties and sanctions.

Thank you.

Appendix A: Biography of Li Yuanlong

Who is Li Yuanlong?
By Laogai Research Foundation

Li Yuanlong was a journalist at *Bijie Daily*, a newspaper in China's Guizhou province. In February 2005, he began to write articles online under the pseudonym Ye Lang (Night Wolf), criticizing living standards and advocating for democracy and free will. He also exposed the dark parts of Chinese society through interviews of the poor and uneducated. Local government officials disapproved and forced him to stop this kind of writing.

Li's troubles began after he published four articles on foreign websites. On September 9, 2005, local police detained him at his office on suspicion of "inciting subversion of state power." On September 23rd, he was placed under house arrest and was formally arrested on the 29th. On July 13, 2006, he was tried, convicted, given a two-year prison sentence, and deprived of political rights for an additional two years.

In September 2007, he was released after serving his jail term. However, life has become harder for him and his family. His reporter status has been revoked and he is barred from working for state entities, including China's state media.

With LRF's help, his son, Li Muzi, was able to come to the U.S. to attend university in 2009. Li Muzi feels obligated to tell Congress about the grave human rights violations they have endured as a result of China's internet censorship.

Li Yuanlong's Verdict

贵州省人民检察院毕节分院指控……被告人李元龙利用"自由门"、"无界浏览"等电脑软件经常上网浏览境外网站。2005年5月至8月期间，李元龙署名"夜狼"或"yehaolang"……在境外网站上，发表了《在思想上加入美国国籍》、《生的平凡 死的可悲》、《不光是涮涮八十老母去世还要继续开会的书记》、《从百岁老朽入党说开去》等四篇文章，捏造、歪曲、夸大有关事实，煽动颠覆国家政权，推翻社会主义制度。（李元龙判决书）

According to the accusation by the Guizhou Provincial People's Procuratorate, Bijie Branch, Defendant Li Yuanlong ... often visits overseas websites by using "Free gate", "UltraSurf," and other such computer software. From May to August 2005, under the pseudonyms of "Ye Lang" (Night Wolf) or "yehaolang", Li Yuanlong published four articles on the overseas websites, namely, "Becoming American, in Ideology," "Ordinary Life, Deplorable Death," ""On the Party Secretary Who Takes a Meeting More Seriously Than His Mother's Death," and "Becoming a Party Member, From the Perspective of an Old Senile Man." These articles fabricated, distorted, or exaggerated the facts, with the purpose of inciting subversion of state power and overthrowing the socialist system. (Li Yuanlong's Verdict)

Appendix A: Biography of Li Yuanlong

本院认为，被告人李元龙在互联网上发表旨在以造谣、诽谤等方式攻击中国共产党的领导，煽动颠覆国家政权的文章，其行为已构成煽动颠覆国家政权罪。公诉机关指控的事实清楚，罪名成立，应予确认。据此，依照《中华人民共和国刑法》第一百零五条第二款、第五十五条及全国人民代表大会常务委员会《关于维护互联网安全的决定》第二条第（一）项之规定，判决如下：

被告人李元龙犯煽动颠覆国家政权罪，判处有期徒刑二年，剥夺政治权利二年。（李元龙判决书）

This Court finds that defendant Li Yuanlong published articles online to attack the CCP leadership and incite subversion of state power by means of slandering and spreading rumors, and what he has done has constituted the crime of inciting subversion of state power. This court also finds that the facts submitted by the public prosecutor are clear and he can be convicted of the crime. In accordance with the second Item of Article 105 and Article 55 of the "Criminal Law," and the first Item of the second paragraph of "The Decision on Safeguarding Internet Security" passed by the National People's Congress Standing Committee, the Court determines the following sentence:

Defendant Li Yuanlong is sentenced to two years imprisonment, plus deprivation of political rights for two years, on charges of inciting subversion of state power. (Li Yuanlong's Verdict)

Appendix B: Biography of Liu Xianbin

Who is Liu Xianbin?
By. Laogai Research Foundation

A victim of China's oppressive authoritarian regime for most of his life, Liu Xianbin has repeatedly spoken out for human rights and democracy while sacrificing his own freedom. Liu and Chinese dissident writers Du Daobin and Zhou Yuanzhi are plaintiffs in a lawsuit against Cisco, Systems Inc., currently pending in Federal Court in Maryland. Over the past decade, Cisco has enabled the Chinese Ministry of Public Security to crack down on dissent through highly sophisticated internet surveillance technology, known as the "Golden Shield Project". Were it not for Cisco's help, the Chinese Communist Party may not have had the tools and technology to persecute, punish and torture Liu for his peaceful and non-violent internet activities.

Born in 1968 in Sichuan Province, Liu Xianbin was attending Renmin University in Beijing when the pro-democracy student movement swept China. He participated in the 1989 protests, including the blocking of military vehicles in Tiananmen Square. Having lost faith in Communist Party rule, Liu helped to organize an anti-communist group and began writing articles criticizing the repression and violent crackdown of the Tiananmen incident and pushing for the establishment of a democratic party. For these "crimes", he was arrested in 1991 and eventually sentenced to 2.5 years in prison on charges of "counterrevolutionary propaganda and incitement," yet this was only the beginning of Liu's activism.

Liu was not deterred by his time in prison and, after his release, he continued advocating for democracy. By 1996, Public Security officials were tracking Liu's activities and movements and brought him in for questioning. He constantly tried to avoid Public Security Bureau officials, but one day, a PSB department chief knocked on his door and took him away, while another officer searched his home. His wife managed to conceal his address book and brought herself to burn her diary, but recalls feeling stripped of her privacy and dignity. Later, when Liu was ill with tuberculosis, the police even came to pay him a visit in the hospital.

In 1998, Liu established the Sichuan branch of the Chinese Democratic Party. Around this time, a police car was stationed outside his home day and night, so Liu was not able to leave in order to print out his writings. Police also closely tracked his internet activity, including all of the articles he published and all of his correspondence. One day he gave his manuscript to his wife to print in a small shop. When the police discovered his writings were again being faxed and distributed, they became suspicious. The Public Security Bureau followed his wife and brought her in for interrogation, and proceeded to confiscate the shop owner's printer and copy machine.

In June of 1999, Liu and his family celebrated his daughter's second birthday. Little did they know this would be their one and only photograph taken together. A month later, the police came to their home and arrested Liu. He spent a month in a detention center before returning home to house arrest. In August, he was convicted of "subversion of

Appendix B: Biography of Liu Xianbin

state power" and sentenced to 13 years in prison with three years' deprivation of political rights.

He was sent to Chuandong Prison in rural Sichuan; his wife and young daughter had to brave treacherous mountain roads in order to visit him. Even then, their visits were limited to half an hour and took place separated by bulletproof glass, always under the supervision of prison guards. Liu spent over nine years in the prison, a laogai forced labor camp, which is home to enterprises like Dazhu Laodong Factory and Automobile Repair Shop.

Around the time of the anniversary of the Tiananmen incident, Public Security Bureau officials brought Liu's wife in for questioning. Because of her unyielding support for her husband, they threatened to remove her from her teaching position in her hometown of Suining and send her to the countryside to teach. While he still remained in prison, the police again came to search his home and again brought his wife in for interrogation and held her in detention overnight. She began to distance herself from friends and family in order to protect them, as simply being affiliated with Liu was enough to get one in trouble with the Public Security Bureau.

Released early for good behavior in 2008, Liu did not give up on his beliefs. He became one of the first signatories to the now famous Charter 08, a petition that calls for democratic reforms, which was authored in part by the now imprisoned Nobel laureate Liu Xiaobo.

Liu continued to publish pro-democracy articles on a number of foreign-run websites, including the Laogai Research Foundation's ObserveChina.net, for which he was arrested on June 28, 2010. On the same day he was detained, the police ransacked his home and confiscated his computer, books, magazines, and data storage devices. This time he was convicted of "inciting subversion of state power". After being held in detention for over eight months, Liu's harsh sentence was handed down- 10 years in prison and deprivation of political rights for two years and four months. The sham trial lasted only two hours; he was not even given the chance to defend himself. His unusually harsh sentence reveals just how afraid the Chinese Communist Party has become of peaceful political dissidents like Liu.

Now reportedly held in Sichuan's Chuanzhong prison, also known as Chengdu Machine Tool Factory, Liu is likely forced to labor alongside the prison's 3,000 inmates, many of whom are serious criminals with life sentences. According to his wife, he has been subjected to harsh treatment, including solitary confinement and torture, because of his refusal to confess his "guilt".

Who is Liu Xianbin? He is a husband and a father. He is a man whose family has been repeatedly torn apart by the Chinese Communist Party. He is a human being who spent 13 of the last 22 years behind bars, and who has spent a mere three years and seven months with his now 14-year-old daughter. He is a peaceful political activist who has,

Appendix B: Biography of Liu Xianbin

time and time again, been forced to make tough decisions that he knew would put his family and his freedom at risk. He is a firm believer in freedom of speech who never gave up on his ideals, and who has made great sacrifices for the sake of the Chinese people, even despite overwhelming pressure to stay silent.

Let Cisco Systems know that their support of the Chinese Communist Party and its efforts to violate the human rights of peaceful political dissidents like Liu Xianbin will no longer be tolerated. To speak out, please contact your elected representatives and sign the Electronic Frontier Foundation's petition— Tell Cisco: Stop helping China abuse human rights!

Liu Xianbin's 2010 Verdict:

From April 2009 to February 2010, Liu Xianbin wrote many articles including, "My Twenty Years in the China Democracy Movement -- The Arrest of Chen Wei, Part 1," "The Street Movement is an Important Part of the Democracy Movement," and "100 Days Out of Jail," and published them on a couple of overseas websites. In these articles, he slandered the Communist regime, saying that it "has been pursuing an oppressive reign of terror", so the Chinese citizens are living, "under the political police's reign of terror," "living like slaves or machines." Liu encouraged "the creation of a powerful opposition group," so that "once the time is right , [it could] quickly become an organization with a fighting spirit," and it could "exert increasingly greater pressure on the authorities, so that the foundation of the ruling class would collapse." All these statements are inciting others to subvert state power and overthrow China's socialist system.

In accordance with the second Item of Article 105, the first Item of Articles 55 and 56, and Articles 66, 71 and 46 of the PRC Criminal Law, as well as "How to Handle the Issues of New Crimes Committed While a Criminal is Serving the Additional Penalty or During the Deprivation of Political Rights" issued by the Supreme People's Court, the Court gives the following sentences:

1. Having committed the crime of inciting subversion of state power, Defendant Liu Xianbin is sentenced to 10 years imprisonment and deprivation of political rights for two years. In addition to this, he must serve the four months and eight days he had not completed before being detained. In total, he has to serve 10 years imprisonment and 2 years and four months' deprivation of political rights;
2. All objects belonging to Liu that was used as evidence in this case shall be confiscated.

Appendix C: Testimony of Liu Xianbin's Daughter

My Father Liu Xianbin and I

----- By Chen Qiao

Mom and Dad were married in 1994.

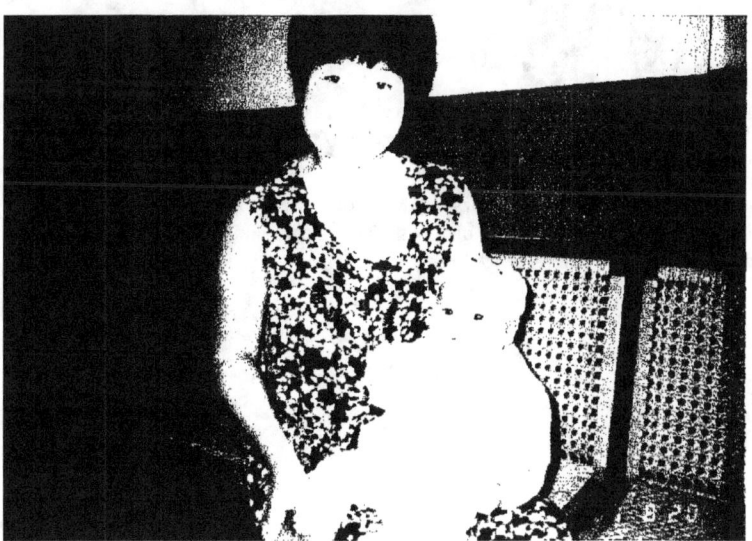

I was born on June 13, 1997.

Appendix C: Testimony of Liu Xianbin's Daughter

My name is Qiao Chen, I'm 14 years old. My father was sent to jail when I was two years old. Therefore, we only have two pictures with the three of us in it. Both of these pictures were taken before I was three.

Appendix C: Testimony of Liu Xianbin's Daughter

This picture was taken on June 20, 1999. Dad was sick on that day. He was taken away 17 days later, and was absent during my childhood.

November 6, 2008, Dad came back home. His daughter had become a beautiful teen girl.

Appendix C: Testimony of Liu Xianbin's Daughter

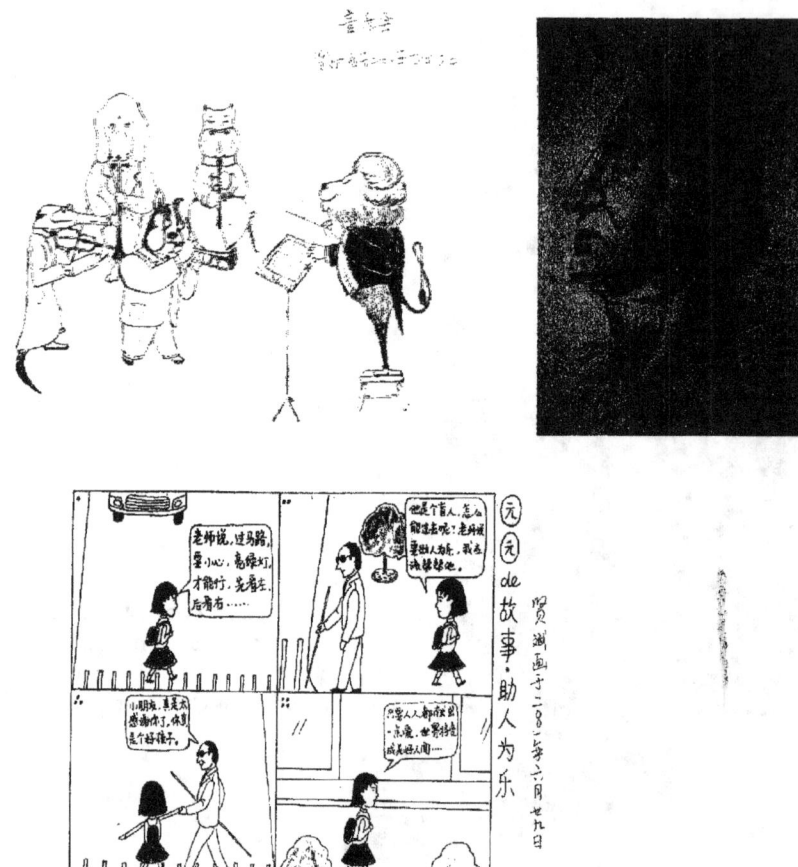

I cannot remember when I took my first trip to visit my dad in jail. Every summer and winter vacation, Mom took me on crowded trains to Nanchong, and from there we took a bus to Dazhu to see my father. We would travel for almost a full day to get there. During that period, Dad regularly wrote me letters. Sometimes, he sent me some comics and drawings that he had drawn. Since he had only a pen, these pictures usually had only one color. When I got them, I colored them in.

During major festivals, like the Spring Festival, Mom and I would write letters to Dad together. This is how the years that Dad had been absent from home slipped by. On December 6, 2008, Dad suddenly came to "my home," but I was already a teenager. I didn't know how to be close with my dad. Perhaps it was because Dad had been absent in my life for a long time, but I felt like a stranger had come into my home. At first, I

45

Appendix C: Testimony of Liu Xianbin's Daughter

wasn't used to having him at home. Fortunately, while we spent those two years together, we got closer and closer. Our relationship gradually returned and we felt more and more comfortable together.

Not long after my 13th birthday, a teacher came to my classroom and asked me to go to the school guardroom. When I got there, I saw two men were already there; they introduced themselves and said that they were police officers. After the head teacher arrived, we started talking. I remember, the head teacher was sitting on my right and the two men were facing us. One of them interrogated me and another took notes. The one who asked me questions was very serious. He ordered me to tell the truth and not lie. I was scared so I immediately agreed.

At first, he asked me some questions like: "What are your hobbies?" "What do you usually do?" and "How do you spend your leisure time?" I gave them the answers. I was confused as to why he brought up those unimportant questions. A moment later, he asked me: "How many computers do you have in your home?" At that time there were two: a desktop for my mom, and a laptop that I shared with Dad. I told the police this. Then he asked: "You two share a laptop? What do you use the laptop for?" At that time, I realized that the reason they came looking for me was related to my dad. I answered: "To surf the internet."

"Doing what?" He asked.

"Listening Music, chatting, watching movies, and reading," I answered.

"Do you write articles?" He asked.

"No, I sometimes write in my diary," I answered.

Then he asked: "What about your dad?"

"He surfs the internet, plays chess, and writes some essays." I said.

"Does he like writing articles?" he asked.

"Yes," I said.

"When does he use the computer?" he asked.

"Pretty much Monday through Friday, while I'm at class. It's mostly him who uses the computer," I said, telling them the truth.

"Are you sure you didn't write any articles on that computer?" he repeated.

"I've written some stories for fun and essays for school," I said.

"Do you know what kind of articles your father writes?" He asked.

"I don't really understand too much about his writings," I said, "I just know one is about the tainted *Sanlu* milk powder."

Then he told me to be more specific about the content of the article. I told him that I forgot, that it was probably an opinion piece.

When the discussion ended, the cops asked me to sign my name in the notebook to prove that these were my words.

When the interrogation was over, classed had already ended. Some of my classmates came to ask me why the cops wanted to see me. I said I didn't know either. At noon, Mom called me. I asked her what happened to Dad; I was worried and crying. Mom comforted me saying: "Don't cry, don't cry, everything is okay!" I believed her and then I felt relieved. I thought the cops were just asking some questions. In the afternoon, I saw

Appendix C: Testimony of Liu Xianbin's Daughter

Mom was waiting for me at the entrance of my dorm (I lived in the dorm on campus). When she saw me she asked, "Are you alright?" I said I was okay, and then I went to school.

I went back home on Friday (I lived in the dorm on weekdays and went back home on weekends). Mom told me Dad was taken away again. Honestly, I did not feel too shaken. He was my dad, but I did not know much about him. Or, for the years in my memory, I did not want to actively get to know him. Moreover, I meant to avoid him sometimes. Before I came over to the US, Mom told me something more about my dad to help me better know and understand him.

Dad is a guest in my life; he comes and leaves in a hurry. His image in my childhood becomes dimmer and dimmer. When I turned 11 years old, he suddenly came back into my life. After living with us for two years, he left so quickly that none of us had time to say goodbye. Actually, I got used to living with just my mom and without my father by my side. So when he went away this time I was not that sad about his leaving. While Dad was gone, Mom raised me to be a healthily and happy teenager. However, when I look back, I feel something is missing in my life.

The life that I am supposed to have is disturbed by an intangible power; it surrounds and frustrates me. While my dad was with me in those two years, I was not willing to get close to him; I was shy and guarded like a hedgehog, not wanting to get too close to him. Now I am full of regret and guilt. I should not have avoided him during that time.

Memories of my dad are hard to recall, but some images come to mind: we played Gobang (*a type of Chinese chess*) together, he taught me The Analects, he asked me to practice fountain pen writing, and he brought me birthday cakes and so on. These moments were not a big deal when they were occurring, but they fill me with warmth now. Now I know memories of these ordinary routines are very dear to Dad and me. In the over 14 years of my life, I only have these two years of precious memories with him.

Not until I came to the US, did I know just how unfairly my dad was treated. Now that I have learned that American companies like Cisco Systems are helping the Chinese police monitor the internet and track down innocent people like my Dad, I do not know what to say. Anyway, I was happy with Mom, but I regret that I did not have Dad in my life. For the last 14 years, I have never said, "I love you" to Dad, but in my heart I know I need him; my mom and I both need him. If he had really done something criminal, then he should be sent to jail. But the truth is, he was sent to the jail by the Communist Party, merely for writing some articles to express his own ideas and opinions. This time, he was sentenced to more than ten years. When he is released, he will have become a 50-year-old man!

My dad is not a great man; he just did something that is right, which should be done by everyone who has a sense of compassion and responsibility. The more I get know my dad, the more I feel that he does not deserve to be sent to jail. Such a thing should not have happened. It has hurt a whole family, a group of people- those who care about my dad, and all those who have a conscience and who refuse to yield!

Cisco & the Ministry of Public Security:
China's Internet Crackdown

Chinese Documents and Translations

*NOTE: Only highlighted portions are translated below

Laogai Research Foundation
1734 20th St NW
Washington DC 20009
Phone: (202) 408-8300
Fax: (202) 408-8302
E-mail: laogai@laogai.org

中国新闻

新闻内容

中国
关于思科
思科新闻
中国新闻
2001年中国新闻
新闻内容

**云南省建设全国第一个基于 IP技术的"三网合一"公安系统广域网
全面采用思科IP技术及服务**

日前，由云南省公安厅建设的全省公安系统综合信息网建成并投入使用，为该省打击犯罪、维护社会治安、提高执法能力提供了保障。该网全面采用思科系统公司基于IP技术的"三网合一"架构及大量思科网络设备，将语音网络和数据网络融为一体，在促进该省公安系统信息高效的同时，极大的节省了长途话费开支，在全国公安系统"金盾工程"信息化建设中起到了良好的示范和带头作用，为实施、推广电子政务"作出了表率作用。

思科系统（中国）网络技术有限公司副总裁林正刚先生对项目的建成表示祝贺，他指出，"电子政务"可以有效提高政府工作效率，进一步提升中国在国际上的形象与地位，实现科技兴国的伟大目标。思科一直致力于国内"电子政务"的建设工作，此次思科IP技术在国内公安系统的成功应用，也是思科为"电子政务"作出了自己的一点贡献。思科将用最好的服务确保网络的正常运行。

公安部有关负责人对云南省公安厅的做法大加赞赏，指出用IP技术建造信息网络不仅先进，为公安机关打击罪犯、维护社会治安、提高办公效率和执法能力，而且可为社会提供信息总服务提供了强有力的支持，作出了"科技强警"的表率，云南省公安厅"三网合一"的做法在其他省公安系统中有很大的推广价值和借鉴经验。

云南省公安厅前期对相关厂商设备的高效性、可靠性、安全性及稳定性等方面进行了认真客观的测试，对竞标方的各种方案开展了广泛的考察和论证后一致认为，采用思科IP技术建造的网络具有统一导证体系，可扩展性强，其独立服务模块化结构可支持多种不同应用，方便开展新业务，良好克服在传统ATM、帧中继技术中存在的诸如网络互操作性差、扩展性及可升级性差、管理维护麻烦等缺点。此外思科IP技术的一个明显优势就是组网速度快，可确保云南省公安综合信息网在最短的时间内建设完成。

思科一举中标的另一个原因是其产品性能高、通用性和稳定性强。作为国际互联网技术的领先厂商，思科拥有建造宽带IP城域网的丰富经验。思科为该项目提供了全赛的SIS 98服务包，可提供7×24小时技术支持，实现设备的三年保修。思科充足的售后服务技术人员、高水平的技术支持和丰富经验为云南省公安厅带来极大的信心。

建成后的云南省公安综合信息网络支持多业务接入，不但可提供高性能的基本数据数据通信、加密传真等等传输业务，还能提供具有一定服务质量保证的增值业务，如分组语音、会议电视系统等，而且可实现远程信息实时查询，开发各类公安业务应用。提供拨号用户的接入和支持拨号备分，增强了整个网络建设的灵活性、扩展性和可靠性，具有优秀的网管功能和多等级QoS、拥塞管理功能。

关于金盾工程：我国公安机关利用现代的信息通信技术，增强统一指挥、快速反应、协调作战、打击犯罪的能力，提高公安工作效率和侦察破案水平，以适应我国在现代经济和社会条件下实现动态管理和打击犯罪的需要，实现科技强警目标的重要举措。"金盾工程"实质上就是公安通信网络与计算机信息系统建设工程。

Yunnan Province Constructs China's First IP-Based "Three-in-One Network"
The Public Security System's WAN Makes Comprehensive Use of Cisco's IP
Technology and Services

July 4, 2001

Yunnan's Public Security Department constructed and began using its province-wide Public Security system integrated information network. This network uses Cisco Systems, Inc.'s IP-based "three-in-one network" framework, as well as large amounts of Cisco networking equipment.

Cisco will provide its best service to guarantee the normal operation of the network.

For this project, Cisco is willing to provide 24/7 technical support.

About the Golden Shield Project: China's public security organs use modern information communication technology to improve its abilities to strengthen its unified command, decrease its response time, coordinate its operations, and fight crime. It will also increase the effectiveness of public security works and surveillance detection levels. In order to adapt to the conditions of China's modern economy and society, it will meet the demands of implementing a dynamic management system and combating criminals, thus reaching the important goal of improving police work through the use of technology. Essentially, the "Golden Shield Project" is a construction project of the public security's communication network and computer information system.

CISCO

中国新闻

新闻内容

2002

新闻内容

思科网络构筑"数字警务"--思科携公安系统网络解决方案亮相"中国大型机构信息化展览会"

在近日举行的首届"中国大型机构信息化展览会"上，思科系统（中国）网络技术有限公司展出了"交通警、刑警移动警务解决方案、社区警务的IP语音解决方案、社会治安防控的视频监控系统、电子学习解决方案"。这是思科积极参与"金盾"工程建设、利用网络解决方案服务公安信息化建设的具体体现，显示出思科作为可信赖的公安系统网络解决方案提供商的卓越实力。思科还为本次展会现场提供了无线局域网平台，让所有参展商和展会观众可随时浏览展会现场情况。

公安人员如何在事故现场及时获得资料和信息支持、并在第一时间解决问题，是目前公安系统面临的重大需求。思科公司此次展出的移动警务解决方案，通过将思科无线方案与思科移动接入路由器的良好结合，配合摄像机、扫描仪等现代化设备，通过移动终端设备，如笔记本电脑和PDA，外出的公安人员就可实现与总部之间的信息共享，随时随地通过电信的无线网络接入到公安外网的数据系统，真正实现了将公安信息网直接延伸到公安干警工作的第一线。

为更好的响应"向素质要警力"的号召，满足各公安分局与省、市各公安系统中人员培训的需求，思科推出的公安系统电子学习解决方案，其最大的特点是接受培训的人员可以针对自己的特点和需求选择培训内容，并且不受时间和地域的限制，降低成本，充分利用资源。不仅可为公安用户节省投资、管理与维护的费用，而且还可以提高公安系统人员的素质和技能。此次展会中，思科公司还展出了与合作伙伴共同开发的完全数字化视频系统，主要应用于省、市公安局的远程监控系统中。而思科IP语音解决方案可为公安/派出所节省投资的费用和管理、维护的开销。

思科中国副总裁兼政府企业事业部总经理张思华指出，作为电子政务建设的重要组成部分，公安系统信息化应用程度是有效地履行维护社会稳定、搞好治安工作的重要保障。思科此次参展出的量身定做的公安系列网络解决方案，可充分满足提高公安机关办公、办案效率的需求，节省开支，加速公安系统信息化进程，加快"数字警务"的进程。

目前，思科公司公安系统解决方案已经在国内公安系统得到广泛应用。其中采用思科全局集中式数据库管理模式建设的深圳市福田区"流动人口管理系统"，在派出所、责任区实现流动人口信息的适时录入、查询、变更，从而实现流动人口动态管理，全面提高了人口管理工作的效率。思科还利用IP语音技术帮助张家港市公安局建设了综合业务通信网络系统，通过IP语音（Voice Over IP）技术，实现了数据与语音的集成传输，提高了网络的整体利用效率，这也是国内公安系统中第一个采用数据、语音集成传输的一体化网络系统。此外，云南省公安局、北京市公安局也纷纷采用思科电子学习及IP语音解决方案进行了网络建设，完全满足了他们在工作中的实际需求。

Cisco Network Builds "Digitalized Police Service System" – With Cisco's Help, Public Security Unveil Its Networking Solutions at the "China Information Infrastructure Expo"

December 5, 2002

At the first ever "China Information Infrastructure Expo", Cisco displayed its "patrolmen, mobile criminal police solution, district police Voice Over IP solution, crime prevention and control video surveillance system, and e-learning solution." This is Cisco's active participation in the construction of the "Golden Shield" project- using network solutions to construct concrete information technologies for the Public Security system. This shows that Cisco is a trustworthy company that provides superior networking solutions for the Public Security system.

Currently, the Public Security system is facing a very important problem. How can Public Security officers at the scene of an accident get timely information and information support and be able to solve the case on their first try? Cisco Systems, Inc. displayed its "mobile police solution", which utilized a fine combination of Cisco's wireless solutions and mobile access routers, paired with video cameras, scanners and other modern equipment that uses mobile terminal equipment- like laptops and PDAs. Dispatched Public Security officers can share information with their headquarters, and can, at any time and at any location, connect to the Public Security's external data system through the wireless telecommunication network. Thus, the Public Security information network will actually be directly connected to the Public Security officers on the front line.

Cisco has designed a Public Security system e-learning solution to fulfill the personnel training needs of each Public Security Bureau (PSB) and each provincial and municipal PSB System. Its greatest feature is that personnel can select training content specifically geared for their unique needs. It is not limited by time or location, it reduces costs and maximizes the use of all resources. Cisco also displayed a completely digitized monitoring system -- which it and its partners developed together -- that mainly uses the remote monitoring system of provincial and municipal PSBs. Moreover, Cisco's Voice Over IP solution can help the PSB and PSB stations reduce investment costs and management, and maintain overheads.

Vice-President and General Manager of Government and Enterprises Division for Cisco's China branch, Zhang Sihua, pointed out that the application of the Public Security system's information technology is an important part of constructing e-government and is effective in maintaining social stability and guaranteeing the improvement of policing. At this expo, Cisco displayed its tailor-made series of network solutions for the Public Security system. It is sufficiently able to improve Public Security organ operations, meet the need to increase the efficiency of solving cases, reduce expenditures, increase the speed at which Public Security system information can be spread, and speed up the construction of the "digitized police service system".

Currently, Cisco's security system solutions are already being widely used in Public Security systems. It has comprehensively improved the efficiency of population management. Cisco also used Voice Over IP technology to help the Zhangjiagang PSB construct an integrated business communications network system. Through its Voice Over IP technology, it was able to achieve the integration of data and voice transmission, and it improved overall network efficiency. This is also the first Public Security system to use the integrated data and voice transmission network system. Additionally, the Yunnan PSB and Beijing PSB are adopting Cisco's e-learning and Voice Over IP technology, one after the other, to construct a network, completely satisfying demands of PSB work.

CISCO

中国新闻

新闻内容

中国
关于思科
思科新闻
中国新闻
2004年中国新闻
新闻内容

筑就最优行业网 服务警务数字化
思科创新技术力助公安部实现对金盾一级网的全面改造
2004年02月24日

为了适应警务现代化建设和改革的需要，进一步推动信息化在警务建设、应用、管理、培训等方面的全面发展，实现科技强警，公安部进一步加大了对"金盾"工程的投资力度。日前，思科系统公司宣布，凭借成熟、先进的整体解决方案和完善的服务，将帮助公安部对金盾一级网设备及联网工程进行全面改造。建成后的网络将集先进性、多业务性、可扩展性及稳定性于一体，不仅可以满足公安系统在宽带网络上同时传输语音、视频和数据的需要，而且还可以支持VPN等业务，完全可以适应新时期公安系统对网络发展和应用的需求。

随着公安系统信息化和"金盾"工程建设的深入发展，以及新时期下新问题、新情况的不断出现，公安系统的网络数据流量和业务量急剧增加。同时，今年也是"金盾"工程建设的关键一年，其目标是建成覆盖全国的公安信息通信网络和涵盖所有公安业务的信息应用系统，并实现以各项公安业务应用为基础，以"数字化警务"为目标的信息共享和综合利用，这无疑对原有金盾一级网提出了巨大挑战。因此，必须进一步发展和完善现有的网络结构，提高网络带宽，以适应新形势下社会治安动态管理的需要。

结合"金盾"工程的实际情况和特点，并在充分考虑当前网络需求以及未来可扩展性的基础上，思科采用GSR12400系列、7609系列路由器及其他相关产品为金盾一级网的改造量身定制了完整的解决方案，在提高产品性能的同时，最大限度地利用了现有网络设备，保护了原有的投资。据了解，改造后的金盾一级网是迄今为止中国所有行业网中应用最为复杂和先进的网络。它改变了常规一级网由中心直接与省网节点连接的结构，而是建立了从中心到八大节点，再由八大节点与其对应二十多个接入节点之间进行连接的二级网结构。同时，它还大大提高了网络带宽，中心与八大节点、八大节点与各接入节点之间的带宽分别达到了622M和155M，可以满足公安系统二十多个业务局、几十种应用系统在该平台上运行。与其他行业网相比，该网络具有结构先进、层次分明、响应速度快等特点，而且其创新的智能网络服务还可以适应未来日益复杂的应用和不断增长的流量对网络的需求。

改造后的网络能否稳定、安全、高效地运行，事关整个社会的安定团结，其重要性不言而喻，因此公安部对合作伙伴的选择极为重视。在与思科公司的长期合作中，思科优质的产品、领先的技术和一流的服务，赢得了公安部的高度认可。此次公安部之所以选择思科，是思科长期以来把有效提高客户的生产效率、保护客户网络建设的投资、实现客户价值的最大化作为公司产品和解决方案的设计目标。此次网络改造项目的成功完成，不仅极大地提高了金盾网络平台的处理能力，方便网络的运行和维护，同时还提升了公安机关打击犯罪、维护社会稳定和公安系统行政管理的能力。

思科中国公司副总裁张思华表示："很高兴与公安部在金盾一级网的建设上展开合作。基于丰富的全球警务网络建设经验和领先的网络解决方案，思科公司将继续为国内公安系统的信息化建设提供全力支持。"

53

Building on the Optimal Industry Network

Cisco's Innovative Technology Force Helps Public Security Bureau to Realize Comprehensive Transformation of Golden Shield's First-Level Network

February 24, 2004

As a means to adapt to the needs of a police force that is undergoing modernization, development, and reform, and to promote the spread of information by strengthening its technology in the areas of police development, application, management and training, the Ministry of Public Security is moving to expand its level of investment in the engineering of the "Golden Shield". Presently, Cisco Systems, Inc. announced that, with its extensive experience, advanced solutions, and high-quality service, it will help the Ministry of Public Security to carry out comprehensive reform of the Golden Shield's first-level network equipment and network engineering. When it is completed, the network will be advanced, multi-service, extensive, and stable. Not only will it be able to meet the Public Security system's needs to simultaneously transmit voice, video and numerical data via broadband networks, but will also be able to support services such as VPN. It can fully adapt to network development and application needs in this new era of Public Security systems.

Following the growth of information technology within the Public Security System, the profound development in the construction of the "Golden Shield" project, and the new problems that arise in this new era, new circumstances constantly emerge. Thus, the Public Security system's network data traffic and work volume have increased dramatically. At the same time, this year has also been a crucial year for the construction of the "Golden Shield" project- the goal of which is to establish a nationwide Public Security information system network that will cover the information application systems for all Public Security affairs. It will also build the foundation of all Public Security service applications and implement information sharing and integrated use with the goal of "digitizing police work". This will undoubtedly be an immense challenge for the original Golden Shield's first-level network. Thus, it is necessary to make progress on the development and improvement of the current network structure, increase the network's bandwidth, adapt to the need for dynamic management of social order in this new situation.

On the basis of combining the real circumstances and characteristics of the "Golden Shield" project and giving sufficient consideration to today's internet demands and future expansiveness, Cisco is using the GSR12400 and 7609 series routers and other related products to create a complete, tailor-made solution for the transformation of Golden Shield's first-level network. While improving the performance of its products, Cisco is maximizing the use of its existing network equipment to protect the original investment. It is understood that, following the

54

transformation of the Golden Shield's first-level network, it will become the most complex and advanced of all Chinese industry networks.

It changed the conventional first-level network by creating a structure that allows the central and provincial network nodes to connect directly to each other. It also established the framework for a second-level network where the core is connected to eight principal nodes, which are further connected to over twenty access points. At the same time, it is still enormously increasing the network bandwidth so that the bandwidth between the core and the eight principal nodes increases to 622 M, while the bandwidth between the eight nodes and the 20 access points increases to 155 M. This is sufficient to meet the demands of over 20 PSBs and enables multiple application systems to run properly on this platform.

Compared to other industry networks, this network has features such as a more advanced, layered structure with a fast response time. Moreover, its innovative, intelligent network service can also adapt to the network demands of increasingly complex applications and constantly increasing traffic.

Whether or not the network will be stable, secure, and highly efficient after its transformation- with regard to the matter of society's stability and unity- it goes without saying, is a matter of great importance. Thus, the Ministry of Public Security also placed great importance on choosing the right cooperative partner. Throughout Cisco System's long-term cooperation, the excellent quality of Cisco's products and its leading technology and first-rate service has won it the high regard of the Public Security Bureau. The reason that the Ministry of Public Security chose Cisco this time is that Cisco has long been efficiently increasing client productivity and protecting its clients' investment in network construction; Cisco's objective is to maximize customer value through its products and solutions.

The successful completion of this network transformation project will not only dramatically increase the processing capabilities of the Golden Shield platform and make operation and maintenance of the network more convenient, but at the same time it will also raise the administrative management capabilities of Public Security organs in taking down criminals and maintaining social stability, as well as the capabilities of the Public Security system.

Cisco Systems, China's Vice-Chairman, Zhang Sihua said, "We are very happy to be cooperating with the Public Security Bureau on the construction of Golden Shield's first-level network. Based on its extensive experience in building global police networks and being a leader in network solutions, Cisco will continue to provide full support for construction of the Ministry of Public Security's informational system.

中国新闻
新闻内容

中国
关于思科
思科新闻
中国新闻
2004年中国新闻

新闻内容

激活二代身份证
思科助公安部架设数字身份高速信息网

2004年09月01日

前不久，公安部开始了对深圳、上海、浙江湖州等三个城市的二代身份证的换发工作，这三个城市是公安部选定的二代身份证的第一批试点城市，而数字身份高速信息网也随之启动。该高速信息网将对二代身份证系统提供有力的支撑和完善的保障，同时提升了公安部对人口身份信息的管理水平，提高了工作效率，拓展了应用。接下来，作为第二批试点城市的北京和天津的居民第二代身份证的换发工作即将展开。到2004年年底，二代身份证将向全国范围的42个省、自治区和直辖市推广。

尽管为了提高防伪性能，第一代身份证在1995年采用了全息塑视塑封套，在一定程度上增加了假冒身份证的仿制难度，但这种身份证仍然存在很多技术缺陷，例如身份证号码偶然性重号、防伪性能差、姓名中的生僻字打不出来、身份证黑片陈旧等，而这些问题都将随着二代身份证发放系统的数字化而解决。更重要的是，第一代身份证的信息基本处于"静止"的状态，无法在全国范围内实施广泛的共享，因此在管理上也存在诸多不便，第二代身份证项目的实施将改变原来的"重发证，轻管理"的现象。为了使身份证信息的管理能够从"静态"管理变成"动态"管理，一个数字化的、安全稳定的高速支撑网的建设迫在眉睫。

通过与思科公司的全面合作，公安部的第一批、第二批试点城市的二代证制证中心机地完成了各中心局域网的建设，其他省、直辖市、自治区制证中心的网络也在谨锣密数的建设中。这样，在各个基层派出所采集的身份证信息并完成汇总后，就可以通过网络传递到制证中心及人口管理处，以快速实现二代身份证的制作和进行有效的管理。

二代身份证作为公安系统网络中的一种应用，该应用的高速支撑网络的建设借鉴了公安系统骨干网的建设方案，事实上，在公安系统的骨干网中，已经大量了采用了思科公司的网络设备。作为全球领先的互联网设备和解决方案供应商，思科公司的产品和技术不但获得了广泛的应用，并且在很多方面得到了有力的证明，比如在安全性方面，有不少用户反应，很多时候，一旦网络感染了病毒，思科的产品一般都不会受到影响，即便受到严重的攻击，也能够很快恢复，这就是它与很多公司产品最不同的地方。

考虑到公安系统网络所要求的安全性、稳定性和可靠性，该散据高速网络采用了思科4507、4506、3725、3550、2950等路由器和交换机产品。这些产品的高安全性和可靠性不仅体现在产品的自身性能上，还表现在能方便的构建整个网络的安全体系：网络级的安全管理功能，加上应用系统进行多级别数据安全管理功能，以及IOS的防火墙特性，提供了内部网络的安全保障，有效阻止非法入侵。同时，思科在这些网络设备的设计中采用了容错技术，保证了应用系统和网络的高可靠运行，并采用高可靠性和扩充性好的产品设计方案，保证了网络长期正常的工作。此外，二代身份证所采集信息的变化，如从黑白照片变成彩色照片，也要求在网络中部署能够支持大量数据交换的内容交换机和存储交换机，而在这方面，思科也提供了性能优良的产品来保证。

56

二代身份证高速信息网建成之后，身份信息将不像原来那样只在公安系统内部使用，而会扩散到社会的相关行业。按照二代身份证的发展目标，这些信息应该是"流动"的，例如买飞机票、登机、过安检；拿着医保卡去医院；去银行办贷款；去邮电局买手机卡等等，只要配有相应的读卡机器，任何一个联网的地方都可以共享身份信息并进行相应的核查。二代身份证的应用将会得到相当大的拓展。

二代身份证的换发是中国自20年前第一代居民身份证面世至以来，对身份证的首次大规模的升级换代工作，是一次里程碑式的事件。同时，也是一个全球最大规模的电子身份证项目，根据计划，将有超过8亿张身份证需要进行发放。该高速网的建设极大的改善了公安部对海量身份信息的管理手段，而且，思科端到端解决方案不仅满足了这个极大规模电子身份证项目当前的业务需要，也为二代身份证未来的应用提供了一个高可靠性、高安全性、高效率、高度集中、开放灵活、低成本、可管理性强的平台。

背景资料
2003年6月28日，第十届全国人民代表大会常务委员会第三次会议上通过了《中华人民共和国居民身份证法》，该法对居民身份证有了新的规定，也为第二代身份证的换发铺平了道路。第二代身份证的意义在于将实现以独立个人为单位进行身份管理，它是个人身份信息数据库化管理的开始。

解决方案	新闻与快讯	社区
	思科新闻	
	博客	
	RSS feeds	
	本地培训与活动	
行业 ＞	网络技术学院	**当地资源**
优惠	Cisco Seminar Series	

**Activating Second Generation ID Cards-
Cisco Aids Public Security Ministry in Constructing Digital ID High-speed
Information Network**

September 1, 2004

Through complete cooperation with Cisco, the Ministry of Public Security (MPS) was able to rapidly construct local area networks (LAN) at second-generation ID card accreditation centers in the pilot cities of Shenzhen, Shanghai, and Huzhou, Zhejiang, as well as in Beijing and Tianjin. The network construction in accreditation centers in other provinces, municipalities and autonomous regions is in full swing. This way, each primary station that collects ID information and completes a summary can pass along this information to accreditation centers and population management offices through this network. This is a faster method of making second-generation ID cards and is improves management efficiency.

In actuality, the backbone of the Public Security system is predominately made up of Cisco networking equipment.

Taking into account the needs of the Public Security system network- namely security, stability and dependability- Cisco's 4507, 4506, 3725, 3550, 2950 routers and switches were chosen to construct this digitized high-speed network.

Cisco's end-to-end solution not only satisfies the current business needs of the largest electronic ID project, but has also provided a dependable, secure, efficient, centralized, open, flexible, low-cost, and highly manageable platform for the future use of the second-generation ID cards.

PREPARED STATEMENT OF XIAO QIANG

NOVEMBER 17, 2011

FROM "GRASS-MUD HORSE" TO "CITIZEN": A NEW GENERATION EMERGES THROUGH CHINA'S SOCIAL MEDIA SPACE

Respectful Chairman, Representative Christopher Smith, Chairman, Cochairman Senator Sherrod Brown, and Distinguished Commission members,

My name is Xiao Qiang. I am the Founder and Chief Editor of bilingual China news website: China Digital Times, and the Principal Investigator of the Counter-Power Lab, at School of Information of UC Berkeley. My research focuses on identifying, documenting and indexing censorship in Chinese cyberspace and generating an online aggregator of censored, blocked and marginalized content. As part of this work, I closely follow the political conversations of Chinese netizens and interpret their coded discourse and terminology.

It is a privilege to speak in front of this important commission alongside my distinguished fellow panelists. My talk today will focus on the intensified and increasingly sophisticated Chinese state control and censorship of the Internet; the growing resistance to such censorship; the expanding online discourse; and the capacity of the Internet to advance free speech, political participation, and social change in China.

1. GOVERNMENT CENSORSHIP

Since the mid-1990s, numbers of Internet users have grown exponentially and by late 2011, there are an estimated 450 million Internet users in China (perhaps tens of millions more if one counts the people who access the web through cell phones). While most of these people use the Web for entertainment, social networking, and commerce, the numbers of netizens engaged in political criticism are steadily growing and are now estimated to be between 10 and 50 million.

The government has employed a multilayered strategy to control and monitor on-line content and activities since the introduction of the Internet in China in 1987. Authorities at various levels use a complex web of regulations, surveillance, imprisonment, propaganda, and the blockade of hundreds of thousands of international websites at the national-gateway level ("the Great Firewall of China").

The government's primary strategy for shaping content is to hold Internet service providers (ISPs) and access providers responsible for the behavior of their customers; thus business operators have little choice but proactively to censor the content on their sites.

Business owners must use a combination of their own judgment and direct instructions from propaganda officials to determine what content to ban. In an anonymous interview with me, a senior manager at one of China's largest Internet portals acknowledged receiving instructions from either State Council Information Office or other provincial-level propaganda officials at least three times a day. Additionally, both the government and numerous websites employ people to read and censor content manually.

Sina Weibo is China's largest Twitter-like microblogging service with 250 million users, according to their own report in late 2011. It is also one of the most tightly controlled spaces on the Chinese Internet and is an example of how control works on various levels. According to one of the company's top executives, "Sina has a very powerful content censorship and infrastructure backup," which includes the ability to automatically monitor its users 24 hours a day while also utilizing hundreds of human monitors.

The same executive noted that monitoring content is Sina's "biggest headache," and entails intensive communication between editors and censors including emails updating the guidelines for monitoring content that are sent every hour. Editors are obligated to report on any "malicious" content, and repercussions for users can include private or public warnings, deletion of content or cancellation of user IDs. Users are rewarded for reporting malicious or pornographic content by clicking a button on the site's homepage. Individual keywords are also filtered on Sina Weibo search; my research group has uncovered over 820 filtered search terms, including "Cultural Revolution," "press freedom" and "propaganda department."

2. NETIZENS' CODED RESISTANCE

The results of government censorship efforts are mixed at best. The government's pervasive and intrusive censorship system has generated equally massive resentment among Chinese netizens. As a result, new forms of social resistance and demands for greater freedom of information and expression are often expressed in coded language and implicit metaphors, which allow them to avoid outright censorship. The Internet has became a quasi-public space where the CCP's dominance is being constantly exposed, ridiculed, and criticized, often in the form of political satire, jokes, videos, songs, popular poetry, jingles, fiction, Sci-Fi, code words, mockery, and euphemisms.

In early 2009, a creature named the "Grass Mud Horse" appeared in an online video that became an immediate Internet sensation. Within weeks, the Grass Mud Horse—or *cao ni ma*, the homophone of a profane Chinese expression—became the de facto mascot of Chinese netizens fighting for free expression. It inspired poetry, videos, and clothing lines. As one blogger explained, the Grass Mud Horse represented information and ideas that could not be expressed in mainstream discourse.

The Grass Mud Horse was particularly suited to the contested space of the Chinese Internet. The government's pervasive and intrusive censorship has stirred resentment among Chinese netizens, sparking new forms of social resistance and demands for greater freedom of information and expression, often conveyed via coded language and metaphors adopted to avoid the most obvious forms of censorship. As a result, the Internet has became a quasi-public space where the CCP's dominance is being exposed, ridiculed, and criticized, often by means of satire, jokes, songs, poems, and code words.

Such coded communication, once whispered in private, is not new to China. Now, however, it is publicly communicated rather than murmured behind the backs of the authorities. For example, since censorship is carried out under the official slogan of "constructing a harmonious society," netizens have begun to refer to the censoring of Internet content as "being harmonized." Furthermore, the word "to harmonize" in Chinese (*hexie*) is a homonym of the word for "river crab." In folk language, *crab* also refers to a bully who exerts power through violence. Thus the image of a crab has become a new satirical, politically charged icon for netizens who are fed up with government censorship and who now call themselves the River Crab Society. Photos of a malicious crab travel through the blogosphere as a silent protest under the virtual noses of the cyber-police. Even on the most vigorously self-censored Chinese search engine, Baidu.com, a search of the phrase "River Crab Society" will yield more than 5.8 million results.

In recent years, Chinese netizens have shown they possess boundless creativity and ingenuity in finding such ways to express themselves despite stifling government restrictions on online speech. This "resistance discourse" steadily undermines the values and ideology that reproduce compliance with the Chinese Communist Party's authoritarian regime, and, as such, force an opening for free expression and civil society in China. At China Digital Times, we have created an online "Grass-Mud Horse Lexicon," or a translated glossary of more than 200 such terms created and spread by netizens in China. Without understanding this coded but widespread (thanks to the Internet) "Grass-Mud Horse Discourse" through the lens of censorship and resistance, one cannot fully understand the contradictions in Chinese society today, and the potential and the possibilities for tomorrow.

3. ONLINE MOBILIZATION

Through online social networks and virtual communities, the Chinese Internet has become a substantial communications platform for aggregating information and coordinating collective action especially through the use of shared language, experiences and images.

For example, this information aggregation process can happen when a local issue resonates with a broader audience and spreads beyond the limited jurisdiction of local officials, sometimes even making it into the national media. When corruption or environmental damage, for example, are exposed, local authorities implicated in the scandal often crack down on news websites hosted within their respective jurisdictions. But when such news finds its way to a website based outside the relevant local jurisdiction, the officials of that jurisdiction will have no means of directly suppressing it. This gap in control between local authorities as well as between local and central authorities opens a space for netizens to transmit information.

Influential bloggers may also mobilize their fellow netizens by acting as spokespersons for certain issue positions, or by giving personal authentication to messages that resonate with the people, or by articulating what others could not say in the face of political censorship. Bestselling author, race-car driver, and blogger Han Han is one such figure. Han is an outspoken critic of government censorship, and his blog posts are often deleted by censors. Nevertheless, his main blog received more than 300-million hits between 2006 and 2009. In April 2010, Time magazine listed Han Han as a candidate for the hundred "most globally influential people." Han Han subsequently wrote a blog post asking the Chinese government "to treat art, literature, and the news media better, not to impose too many restrictions and censorship, and not to use the power of the government or the name of the state to block or slander any artist or journalist." This post generated some 25,000 comments from his readers and was viewed by more than 1.2 million people. The article has also been widely reposted online; in May 2010, a Google search found more than 45,000 links reposting all or part of the essay. Despite official efforts to use the Great Firewall to block Chinese netizens from voting for Han Han on Time's website, he came in second in the final tally, showing the mobilizational power of his writing.

4. ROLE OF SOCIAL MEDIA TECHNOLOGIES AND AMERICAN COMPANIES

It is not just Han Han's words that are so influential, but the social media technologies – search, file-sharing, RSS, blogging, microblogging, image and video-sharing, social networking, etc – that allow them to spread freely, despite government censorship.

On November 2, 2011, the State Council of Information Office issued directives to all national and local websites: "Thoroughly delete all information and commentaries about Ai Weiwei's "borrowing money to pay tax" event." This refers to the penalty of a $2.4 million back tax bill levied on dissident artist Ai Weiwei, who spent three months in jail this spring. Through the Internet, Ai called for loans from supporters around the world to pay the bill. Searching on Sina Weibo, one will found over a dozen words and phrases relating to "Ai Weiwei" have been recently blocked, and many such posts were soon deleted; however Ai Weiwei's call for loans has been reposted by devoted readers, and circulated through emails, instant chats, closed forums and private messages among users on a variety of social networking services. Ten days after the censor's decisive directive, days, about 30,000 people had sent in a combined total of 8.7 million yuan ($1.37 million) to pay Ai Weiwei's penalty, despite the state censor's full efforts to suppress his words from spreading.

This is what China's leaders most fear: the power of truth-telling among the Chinese population, which directly challenges their privilege, ideological control, and the legitimacy of the regime. The Chinese government has learned that it can't merely target Internet users, but must focus on information technologies, access to the network, and the companies that provide these tools.

That's where American Internet companies enter the story. Because American Internet companies are not under the control of the government and therefore cannot be trusted to abide by the government's rules, they are most often prevented from entering the market on a level playing field, or simply blocked by the Great Firewall. Several top global websites, including Google, YouTube, Twitter, and Facebook, as well as thousands of other websites, are no longer easily accessible. China's intrusive government policies effectively mark the beginning of a cyberworld divided into the internet and the "Chinternet", with the Great Firewall marking the boundary.

5. EMERGENT NEW POLITICAL IDENTITY

The Chinese government has the determination, resources and technology to make the Internet work in support of its ruling status quo. However, its dominance is constantly being contested by netizens' online civil disobedience and public demands for rights. The result of such interplay of censorship and digital resistance is an emerging pattern of public opinion and citizen participation that represents a shift of power in Chinese society. The Internet allows citizens to comment on certain (albeit limited) topics, and create their own shared discourse which is outside the bounds of government censorship and propaganda. In addition, an entire generation of online public agenda setters has emerged to become influential opinion leaders. I have observed a remarkable phenomenon that many of the most influential online opinion leaders appear to hold in common values supporting democracy, human rights and freedom of expression. These netizens, with their growing numbers, expanding social networks, political resilience, and increasing influence, seem to be evolving from "voices under domination" to "universal values advocates." This new, emerging generation of "Internet citizens" is becoming one of the most dynamic forces in setting the media agenda and fostering civil engagement on public issues in China, despite the government's control efforts. This new generation—embodying alternative (liberal, democratic) political values and connected through the Internet—will certainly change China's future course.

6. RECOMMENDATIONS TO THE US GOVERNMENT

Increasing funding to projects which aim to expand the free flow of information on the Internet, such as (1) projects which monitor Internet censorship, identify and archive censored content and make such contents re-accessible for netizens (2) development and deployment of counter-censorship technologies in support of online civil society, human rights and journalism communities in China and other countries with a censored Internet.

Thank you, Mr. Chairman.

———

PREPARED STATEMENT OF GILBERT B. KAPLAN

NOVEMBER 17, 2011

INTRODUCTION

China's censorship of the Internet and its restrictions on the free flow of information have a very significant impact on U.S. economic and trade interests. China continues to impose debilitating burdens on foreign Internet service providers through its censorship regime, its blocking of foreign websites, and its "Great Firewall" infrastructure, which inhibit or prevent all together U.S. companies' ability to do business in China, and their ability to compete with Chinese domestic companies. China's Internet service providers have capitalized on this discriminatory treatment of U.S. companies and have consequently experienced great success. Earlier this year, for example, RenRen (known as "China's Facebook") filed for a U.S. public offering, symbolizing its success to date and its plans for expansion.[1] Meanwhile, Facebook is blocked in China. These measures have been ongoing for years, and have had an

---

[1] http://money.cnn.com/2011/04/18/technology/renren—IPO/?section=money—latest

overwhelming adverse impact on market share for U.S. companies—perhaps to the extent that such market share can never be recovered.

China's blocking and filtering measures, and the fog of uncertainty surrounding what China's censors will and will not permit, violate numerous of China's international obligations, including provisions of the WTO General Agreement on Trade and Services ("GATS") and China's WTO Protocol of Accession.

The negative impact of these violations on America's premier Internet companies is profound. There are several corporate victims of China's exclusionary practices. Although there is public information identifying several large companies that have been blocked or restricted by the Great Firewall, including YouTube, Facebook, Twitter, Vimeo, Google, and the Huffington Post, to name a few, there are many other companies that have been blocked from access in China that I am not able to identify by name specifically because these companies fear retaliation. These companies come from various sectors, including energy, labor mediation, tourism, education, web hosting, and advertising, among others. The fact that these large, well-established companies and other fast-growing U.S. firms, so successful in every other major market in the world, are reluctant to come forward with specific information that would form the basis of a WTO complaint against the Chinese government is powerful testament to (1) the importance of the Chinese Internet market—the largest in the world—to these firms' continued success, and (2) the risk of retaliation that these firms face if they are seen as lending direct support to a trade complaint against China. Moreover, companies not yet in existence, but for which China could represent a significant business opportunity, do not even have a voice in the matter and perhaps never will.

I represent the First Amendment Coalition, an award-winning, non-profit public interest organization dedicated to advancing free speech for individuals and companies just like those denied access to China's Internet market. I have been working with them to address the issue of China's Internet restrictiveness since 2007. The issues regarding internet censorship and internet blockage are trade issues cognizable under the WTO, as well as freedom of speech issues. They are a harmful trade barrier to U.S. business which must be ended.

The First Amendment Coalition was able to persuade the Office of the U.S. Trade Representative ("USTR") to take the critical step of requesting detailed information from China on its internet restrictions under Article III:4 of GATS, which mandates transparency in a Member's application of measures affecting services. GATS Article III:4 reads as follows.

> Each Member shall publish promptly and, except in emergency situations, at the latest by the time of their entry into force, all relevant measures of general application which pertain to or affect the operation of this Agreement.

USTR's request to China follows a three year effort by the First Amendment Coalition to get the U.S. government to take a tough stance to address China internet restrictions in violation of international trade rules, free speech, and human rights. The U.S. request to China under GATS Article III:4 is highly significant not only because it is the very first time any WTO Member has utilized that provision of the GATS agreement, but also because it is the first time that the U.S. government, or any country, has made a formal submission through the WTO to China to address internet censorship.

Contrary to GATS Article III:4, China's measures with respect to Internet services have not been published promptly, and in fact, the blocking and filtering measures have not been published at all.[2] In this regard, we have been unable to document written directives or specific governmental instructions concerning China's measures constituting the "Great Firewall," but this in effect lends support to the argument that China is not transparent in its practices related to controlling and censoring Internet content. Indeed, China has published few, if any, regulations related to Internet services. The Chinese government recently issued an official decision, currently available only in Chinese, which appears not to contain "any new concrete

---

[2] A panel has previously interpreted the term "publish" in the WTO Agreements as more than "making publicly available." In Chile-Price Band System and Safeguard Measures Relating to Certain Agricultural Products, the panel held that the requirements to publish a report in the Agreement on Safeguards meant "to make generally available through an appropriate medium." Appellate Body Report, Chile-Price Band System and Safeguard Measures Relating to Certain Agricultural Products, WT/DS207/AB/R (adopted 23 October 2002), para. 7.128. Further, "[t]he obligation is of an absolute character and due diligence obliges WTO members to publish more, rather than less, because of the terms 'relevant' and 'affecting' invite a wide reading." Mitsuo Matsushita, Thomas J. Schoenbaum, & Petros C. Mavroidis, The World Trade Organization, Law, Practice, and Policy (2003).

policies but it does set the stage for future moves to rein in parts of the Internet at the possible expense of the commercial Internet companies."[3]

The historic action taken by USTR is also a significant and important step because, in addition to promoting transparency and free speech, it may result in China providing information in response to U.S. questions that will assist small and medium-sized U.S. businesses in entering the Chinese market, which they currently are unable to do given the lack of certain vital information involving use of the Internet. As USTR indicated in its press release,

> [a]n Internet website that can be accessed in China is increasingly a critical element for service suppliers aiming to reach Chinese consumers, and a number of U.S. businesses, especially small- and medium-sized enterprises, have expressed concerns regarding the adverse business impacts from periodic disruptions to the availability of their websites in China.

Small and medium-sized U.S. businesses are particularly disadvantaged by China's Great Firewall because, unlike bigger U.S. companies, they do not have the resources to physically set up shop in China so they are simply excluded from the Chinese market.

Some of the information requested from China by USTR included the following:

• With respect to China's rules governing website blocking: Who is responsible for determining when a website should be blocked? What are the criteria for blocking access? Where are the guidelines published? Who does the actual blocking? How can a service supplier know if their website has been blocked? Are decisions to block appealable? Is the process used to prevent access the same or different for foreign and domestic content?

• With respect to the State Internet Information Office ("SIIO") established by the State Council: What are the responsibilities and authorities of SIIO? Will SIIO handle licenses, approval processes, and questions on filtering and other laws?

• With respect to inadvertent blocking where one site is blocked when it shares an IP address with a website China has deemed harmful: How does it occur? Can it be avoided? Will Chinese authorities notify the owner of the web hosting service so that it may ensure other sites are not inadvertently blocked? How can companies resolve inadvertent blocking?

• With respect to the broad nature of the eleven categories of content which Internet service providers may not disseminate:[4] Are there any criteria to determine when content falls within the eleven categories? Are government requests to filer specific terms communicated directly to Internet information service providers? Are the same terms subject to filtering made available to Internet information service providers inside and outside of China?

• With respect to the prevention of "illegal information" as that term is used in the White Paper on the Internet in China: How is illegal information defined? Is a written government order required for a private corporation or relevant authority to block the transmission of illegal information? What types of technical measures are service suppliers expected to use to prevent transmission of the illegal information? Are the technical measures to block illegal information applied automatically to domestic and foreign traffic? If not, how are they applied? Does Internet content from outside of China go through a separate monitoring process for illegal information than Internet content created inside of China? If so, how do they differ?

---

[3] See "6th Plenum Report Suggests China Will Strengthen Internet Management," Digicha Internet and Digital Media in China, October 26, 2011, citing from the "Central Committee Decision Concerning the Major Issue of Deepening Cultural System Reforms, Promoting the Great Development and Prosperity of Socialist Culture" from the 6th Plenum of the 17th Communist Party Congress (currently available only in Chinese), available at http://digicha.com/index.php/2011/10/6th-plenum-report-suggests-china-will-strengthen-internet-management/.

[4] According to measures issued by China's State Council, Internet services providers may not disseminate information with content that: (1) opposes the fundamental principles determined in the Constitution; (2) compromises state security, divulges state secrets, subverts state power or damages national unity; (3) harms the dignity or interests of the state; (4) incites ethnic hatred or racial discrimination or damages inter-ethnic unity; (5) sabotages state religious policy or propagates heretical teachings or feudal superstitions; (6) disseminates rumors, disturbs social order or disrupts social stability; (7) propagates obscenity, pornography, gambling, violence, murder or fear or incites the commission of crimes; (8) insults or slanders a third party or infringes upon the lawful rights and interests of a third party; (9) disturbs the public order by instigating illegal gatherings, associations, parades, demonstrations, or assemblies; (10) organizes activities in the name of illegal civil organizations; contains other content prohibited by the laws and administrative regulations, or by the state.

We hope and expect that the Government of China will answer these questions fully and promptly, fulfilling its obligations under the WTO to maintain an open internet and not discriminate against U.S. business.

The remainder of this submission will review in greater detail the Internet restrictions in China, the adverse trade impact caused by those restrictions, and how those restrictions would appear to violate China's international trade obligations.

I. CHINA'S INTERNET RESTRICTIONS

U.S. and foreign Internet companies have faced a long history of discriminatory treatment in China, to their disadvantage and to the advantage of their Chinese competitors. China has for many years maintained a policy, popularly known as the "Great Firewall," under which it has exerted strict control over the use of the limited system of fiber optic cables that connects networks in China to the outside world. As we understand it, China has installed certain hardware, known as "tappers" or "network sniffers," at each entry point so that when a user in China attempts to access a good or service located on a server outside of China, the tappers create mirror copies of the data packets that flow back and forth between the two servers, and the mirror copies are delivered to a set of computers that automatically review the data packets. The computers can be, and often are, pre-progammed to block a particular domain name server ("DNS"), Internet Protocol ("IP") address, or Universal Resource Locator ("URL") address.[5]

The government of China ("GOC") also employs tens of thousands of individuals whose sole mission is to search the Internet for objectionable content. Their work often results in the blocking of additional DNS, IP, and URL addresses.[6]

Following USTR's Article III:4 request, China defended its Internet censorship as an effort to "safeguard the public."[7] Although the ruling Communist Party claims its monitoring and blocking is to promote "constructive" websites, stop the spread of "harmful information," and develop what it calls a healthy internet culture, it is unclear what content is subject to blocking and often the blocked content has nothing resembling "harmful information."[8] Additionally, the blocking appears motivated by other competitive or political agendas. For example, access to the Android Marketplace was blocked within China just after Google announced it would help the Dalai Lama to visit South Africa virtually.[9]

II. HARM CAUSED BY CHINA'S RESTRICTIONS

Chinese internet restrictions have disadvantaged American businesses, to the benefit of Chinese businesses. According to news reports, Facebook and Twitter, for example, have been blocked in China. In their absence, copycat websites based in China (with censored content) have been able to flourish. It seems unlikely that Facebook and Twitter will be able to regain the market share lost to their Chinese competitors even if they were unblocked at some point in the future. Chinese users have already developed a preference for certain social media sites, and it is doubtful that they would have an incentive to switch services.[10] The loss of a huge potential

---

[5] See e.g., "12VPN and Other VPN Services DNS Poisoned by Great Firewall in China," June 27, 2011, available at http://www.bestvpnservice.com/blog/12vpn-now-dns-poisoned-in-china-by-great-firewall; "Google+ Now DNS Blocked in China," July 5, 2011, available at http://www.isidorsfugue.com/2011/07/google-now-dns-blocked-in-china.html; "China Strengthens Great Firewall, While, Chinese Bypass It," March 3, 2011, available at http://www.bestvpnservice.com/blog/china-strengthens-great-firewall-while-chinese-bypass-it; "Ahead of Party Anniversary, China Poisons the Internet," July 1, 2011, available at http://uncut.indexoncensorship.org/2011/07/ahead-of-party-anniversary-china-poisons-the-internet/.

[6] See "You've Got Mail," Time Magazine, October 16, 2011, available at http://www.time.com/time/magazine/article/0,9171,2096818,00.html

[7] "Beijing leaps to defense of 'Great Firewall of China,'" Reuters, October 20, 2011, available at http://www.reuters.com/article/2011/10/20/us-china-internet-idUSTRE79J1PU20111020.

[8] See "6th Plenum Report Suggests China Will Strengthen Internet Management," Digicha Internet and Digital Media in China, October 26, 2011, citing from the "Central Committee Decision Concerning the Major Issue of Deepening Cultural System Reforms, Promoting the Great Development and Prosperity of Socialist Culture" from the 6th Plenum of the 17th Communist Party Congress (currently available only in Chinese), available at http://digicha.com/index.php/2011/10/6th-plenum-report-suggests-china-will-strengthen-internet-management/.

[9] "Android Marketplace blocked by Great Firewall of China," The Register, October 10, 2011, available at http://www.theregister.co.uk/2011/10/10/china—android—blocking/.

[10] See, e.g., Lin Shujuan, Flutter over New Twitter, China Daily (Oct. 22, 2009) http://www.chinadaily.com.cn/cndy/2009–10/22/content—8829406.htm (discussing the rise in popularity of Sina Weibo, a microblogging website with monitored content, since Twitter became inaccessible in China); Glen Loveland, When Will China Unblock Facebook and Twitter? (Sep. 28, 2009) http://www.examiner.com/x-/x-15615–Asia-Headlines-Examinery2009m9d28–When-will-China-

Continued

64

market for these companies indicates the extent of the harm caused by the Chinese actions. In addition to the direct loss of access to Chinese consumers by these companies comes the loss from all of the advertisers that would ordinarily be offering their services on the Internet pages of these social media service providers.

The number of Internet users in China has exceeded 500 million, growing at double digit rates since 2008, roughly twice the size of the U.S. market, which grew only 2.5 to 4.5 percent in the same timeframe. China is now the largest market for Internet users [11] and U.S. businesses are effectively being blocked from or only given highly restricted access to that market. U.S. companies excluded from the Chinese market are not just large tech companies but small and medium businesses including "travel sites, engineering firms and consulting firms, which have found their sites blocked and have complained to the trade office." [12] A 2011 report by the McKinsey Global Institute estimates that there is a ten percent increase in productivity for small and medium businesses from internet usage.[13] This productivity growth is denied U.S. companies that are blocked from providing their services in China.

U.S. companies are subject to the strict controls that completely disrupt their service, or at a minimum seriously delay the transmission of information. Users of these websites, if they actually endure the wait and do not move to a competitor service supplier,[14] suffer from a decrease in the quality of service, causing commercial harm to U.S. companies.[15]

It would be very useful for this Commission to undertake, directly or perhaps through an economic consulting firm, an economic analysis of the overall harm caused to U.S. companies by the Chinese blockage and censorship of the internet. I think that would be one useful follow-up to this hearing.

III. CHINA'S INTERNET RESTRICTIONS VIOLATE ITS INTERNATIONAL TRADE OBLIGATIONS

The Chinese Government's actions appear to constitute various violations of WTO agreements to which China is a party, particularly the GATS Agreement. The Chinese actions in question, although often based on unwritten policies and practices, would still constitute "measures" that can be challenged under the World Trade Organization Dispute Settlement procedures. In this regard, the Appellate Body and various WTO panels have confirmed that actionable "measures" subject to WTO dispute settlement include not only written laws and regulations, but other government actions as well.[16] Panels have also recognized the subtleties of government pressure on private companies as "measures" that may be challenged at the WTO.[17]

In addition to USTR's current GATS Article III:4 request, there are more aggressive steps that the United States could take to protect its vital economic interests. While we believe that China currently is preparing its official response to USTR's Article III:4 request, if China fails to respond or fails to respond meaningfully, the United States would then have a readily apparent basis to initiate formal dispute settlement proceedings in the WTO. Paragraph 1 of GATS Article XXIII says "[i]f

unblock-Facebook-and-Twitter ("Every Chinese user who can't use the site is that much more likely to turn to China's domestic copycat, YouKu"); China's Twitter Clones, Read Write Web (Mar. 5, 2010) http://www.readwriteweb.com/archives/china—twitter—clones.php (quoting Chinese technology writer Kaiser Kuo: "Although there would be an uptake in the number of users on Twitter, if it was ever to be made available again, Weibo and others will have gained too much momentum by then").

[11] "U.S., China Clash Over Internet Great Wall," China-U.S. Trade Law, October 31, 2011, available at http://www.chinaustradelawblog.com/2011/10/articles/trade-disputes/wto/us-china-clash-over-internet-great-wall-acaaeaecea/.

[12] "China tangles with Internet access," Politico, citing USTR official, October 30, 2011, available at http://www.politico.com/news/stories/1011/67190.html.

[13] Internet Matters: The Net's Sweeping Impact On Growth, Jobs, and Prosperity, McKinsey Global Institute, May 2011, available at http://www.mckinsey.com/mgi/publications/internet—matters/pdfs/MGI—internet—matters—full—report.pdf.

[14] "Android Marketplace blocked by Great Firewall of China," The Register, October 10, 2011, available at http://www.theregister.co.uk/2011/10/10/china—android—blocking/.

[15] See e.g., "Can China's Economy Thrive with a Censored Internet?" Time, October 26, 2011, available at http://curiouscapitalist.blogs.time.com/2011/10/26/can-china%E2%80%99s-economy-thrive-with-a-censored-internet/.

[16] See, e.g., Appellate Body Report, United States – Sunset Review of Anti-Dumping Duties on Corrosion-Resistant Carbon Steel Flat Products from Japan, WT/DS244/AB/R (adopted Jan. 9, 2004), paras. 81–85 ("In principle, any act or omission attributable to a WTO Member can be a measure of that Member for purposes of dispute settlement proceedings".) (The Appellate Body also referred to its earlier opinion in Guatemala–Cement I (AB), which stated that " ... a 'measure' may be any act of a Member, whether or not legally binding, and it can include even non-binding administrative guidance by a government.").

[17] Panel Report, Japan – Measures Affecting Consumer Photographic Film and Paper, WT/DS44/R (adopted Apr. 22, 1998), para. 10.44.

any Member should consider that any other Member fails to carry out its obligations or specific commitments under this Agreement, it may with a view to reaching a mutually satisfactory resolution of the matter have recourse to the dispute settlement understanding."

In addition to a potential violation under GATS Article III on transparency, there are other WTO obligations that China appears to violate with its Internet restrictions, including other GATS provisions, as is discussed below.

Initiation of a WTO dispute settlement proceeding against Chinese Internet restrictions by the United States would signal to the U.S. business community, to consumers around the world, and to China, that the U.S. government will assert its rights under WTO agreements when China fails to fulfill its WTO obligations, even in those areas that may be of a more sensitive nature. Unfortunately, these sensitivities give rise to a number of obstacles to U.S. initiation and prosecution of a formal WTO dispute against China.

As noted, it is difficult to find companies willing to come forward to support a potential case against China for fear of retaliation. Due to this fear, specific facts needed by the U.S. government to support many claims under the WTO are difficult to document. In addition, also as noted, many of the Chinese laws, regulations, policies, and practices regarding Internet services are not written down, although they are enforced de facto.[18]

A. China's Internet Censorship Violates Other Provisions Of GATS

China made specific commitments regarding market access and national treatment for services in various service sectors.[19] China's Internet policies would appear to violate many of these specific commitments under the GATS, including in the areas of Data Processing Services, Photographic Services, Telecommunication Services, Mobile Voice and Data Services, Audiovisual Services, Tourism and Travel Related Services, and Transport Services. By pursuing these policies, China denies market access to U.S. companies and discriminates against the services of U.S. companies in favor of Chinese companies.

Although U.S. companies offer a wide range of services over the Internet, four service sectors that would appear to suffer disproportionately under Chinese policies are: (1) Advertising services (the primary revenue source for U.S. suppliers of Internet-based services, particularly those operating search engines, social networking, and data/photo sharing, is through advertising and U.S. services suppliers obtain revenue from the development and posting of targeted advertisements on their webpages and facilitating access to other websites by their users clicking on the advertisements); (2) Data processing and tabulation services (relevant U.S. services suppliers are providing consumers with the ability to access certain tools over the Internet that enable them to make, edit, and share videos or photos, or other data and that allow them to search for content on other websites and the U.S. services supplier is necessarily processing data for the consumer and providing a tool to access defined data bases or the Internet generally); (3) On-line information and database retrieval; and (4) Videos, including entertainment software and (CPC 83202), distribution services ("Video/entertainment distribution services").

There follows below a brief discussion of some of the specific GATS claims that might be made against the Chinese measures in question and some of the factors that would need to be considered in prosecuting such claims.

1. National Treatment

China's restrictions on U.S. Internet companies appear to violate the national treatment provision in Article XVII of the GATS, which provides that "each Member shall accord to services and service suppliers of any other Member, in respect of all measures affecting the supply of services, treatment no less favourable than that it accords to its own like services and service suppliers."

The Chinese measures at issue would seem to fall within one or more of at least four services subsectors for which China has inscribed a specific commitment, without limitation on national treatment, in its WTO Services Schedule. As such, China's measures must comply with the obligations in Article XVII for these subsec-

---

[18] See US – Zeroing (EC) at paras. 192, 198.

[19] These commitments appear in an addendum to the Working Party Report on the Accession of China and are an integral part of the GATS. Report of the Working Party on the Accession of China, Addendum, Schedule CLII—The People's Republic of China, Part II—Schedule of Specific Commitments on Services List, List of Article II MFN Exemption, WT/MIN(01)/3/Add.2 (10 Nov 2001) ("Schedule of Specific Commitments").

tors.[20] Current Chinese treatment of U.S. Internet companies, including filtering and blocking through the "Great Firewall" and mandated disabling of certain service functions, modifies the conditions of competition in favor of Chinese suppliers such as Baidu (considered the "Google" of China); as such, these measures are inconsistent with Article XVII of the GATS.

If China's measures were challenged in a WTO proceeding, a Panel would first determine whether China's measures are indeed "affecting" the supply of these services. As noted by the Appellate Body in EC—Bananas III:

> [T]he term of "affecting" reflects the intent of the drafters to give a broad reach to the GATS. The ordinary meaning of the word "affecting" implies a measure that has "an effect on", which indicates a broad scope of application. This interpretation is further reinforced by the conclusions of previous panels that the term "affecting" in the context of Article III of the GATT is wider in scope than such terms as "regulating" or "governing." [21]

It is therefore not necessary for China's measures to be directly regulating or governing the business of U.S. Internet service providers, but merely that the measures have an effect on these services, and their providers' ability to do business in China. China's measures clearly have "an effect on" these services—indeed, a very detrimental one.[22]

Second, the United States would need to demonstrate that China's measures accord "less favorable" treatment to U.S. suppliers than to China's domestic suppliers of "like" services. As set forth in GATS Article XVII:3, the test for less favorable treatment is whether the measure "modifies the conditions of competition in favor of services or service suppliers of" China compared to like services or services suppliers of the United States.[23] Persuading a panel in this regard would require the production of extensive data and specific information demonstrating the competitive disadvantage suffered by U.S. companies due to China's measures. A comparison of blockages of websites, upload times for content of websites, and other significant impediments to Internet service providers would likely reveal significant and swift loss of market share by U.S. providers.

2. Market Access

Article XVI:2 of the GATS prohibits Members from maintaining or adopting quantitative limitations on service operations or service output. China's restrictions on certain U.S. Internet companies' services constitutes a de facto quantitative limitation on such services, therefore violating this provision.

3. Domestic Regulation

Under Article VI of the GATS, for services sectors in which specific commitments have been undertaken, China must administer its measures in a "reasonable, objective and impartial manner" and, for all services sectors, must ensure that tribunals or procedures are available for the prompt review and remedy of administrative decisions. China's restrictions on U.S. Internet companies are subjective and non-transparent, and there are no tribunals or procedures for the review of these administrative decisions. The restrictions therefore violate China's obligations under Articles VI:1 and VI:2(a) of the GATS.

China's "Great Firewall" filtering and blocking practices would also seem to violate the GATS Annex on Telecommunications, which states in paragraphs 4 and 5 that "each Member shall ensure that relevant information on conditions affecting access to and use of public telecommunications transport networks and services is publicly available" and that "[e]ach Member shall ensure that any service supplier of any other Member is accorded access to and use of public telecommunications transport networks and services on reasonable and non-discriminatory terms and

---

[20] In the case of potential market access violations in relation to telecommunications services, the United States will need to address potential Chinese arguments that the measures are non-discriminatory and are based on China's right, under the footnote in its schedule, to require that such services be channeled through approved gateways. Moreover, in relation to national treatment for video/entertainment distribution services, China has not scheduled any limitation in relation to "content review" and thus discriminatory content review would not be justified by any reservation or limitation.

[21] Appellate Body Report, European Communities—Regime for the Importation, Sale and Distribution of Bananas, WT/DS27/AB/R (adopted 25 September 1997), para. 220.

[22] See "Enabling Trade in the Era of Information Technologies: Breaking Down Barriers to the Free Flow of Information," Google paper released November 15, 2010, available at http://static.googleusercontent.com/external—content/untrusted—dlcp/www.google.com/en/us/googleblogs/pdfs/trade—free—flow—of—information.pdf.

[23] See, e.g., Panel Report, Canada – Certain Measures Affecting the Automotive Industry, WT/DS139/R, WT/DS142/R (adopted 19 June 2000), para. 10.80.

conditions." In addition, paragraph 5(c) imposes an obligation on China to ensure that U.S. services suppliers may use the public telecommunications transport networks and services "for the movement of information within and across borders" and "for access to information contained in data bases or otherwise stored in machine-readable form" in the United States or in the territory of another WTO Member. China's filtering and blocking on Internet content clearly restricts the availability of these telecommunications networks in a discriminatory fashion.

CONCLUSION

We appreciate the Commission holding this hearing and inviting me to testify. We also appreciate the efforts of USTR in submitting the GATS III:4 questions. We urge the Commission to take into account our views in its ongoing work on this issue. We also urge the Commission to monitor China's responses to these questions as well as USTR's continuing efforts on this very important issue. An open and accessible internet in China is a prerequisite to U.S. success in the Chinese market, and a goal that we must continue to fight for until it is achieved.

PREPARED STATEMENT OF ED BLACK

NOVEMBER 17, 2011

Chairman Smith and Chairman Brown, I appreciate the opportunity to again testify before the Commission to discuss China's censorship of the Internet. I am President and CEO of the Computer & Communications Industry Association (CCIA), an organization that has promoted openness, competition, and free trade for over 35 years.

I commend the Commission for examining the prescient issue of how restrictions on the free flow of information online pose not only significant human rights concerns, but economic concerns as well. CCIA has long been an advocate of openness online, as we ardently believe that freedom and openness are not only at the heart of our industry's rapid growth, but are also the core values underpinning our success as a democracy.

I know that traditionally freedom of expression has rightly been viewed through the lens of human rights, and I strongly support working through the United Nations and NGOs to put pressure on recalcitrant members of the international community who defy their commitments in this arena. We deeply admire the courage and sacrifice of activists such as Mr. Li's father and Pastor Zhang who seek freedom for their people. As their prior testimony makes clear, the human toll of such measures is enormous. A commitment to freedom, particularly the freedom of expression, is the keystone of our nation and has premeditated our foreign policy since America's incipiency. It is also what has driven so many Tunisians, Egyptians and Syrians to sacrifice their lives in recent months. I firmly believe that the United States must continue its full-throated support of freedom of expression worldwide—both online and offline. In fact, some of our biggest domestic and foreign policy mistakes occurred when we have overlooked these principles in the name of diplomatic or political expediency. In this vein, I support our State Department's efforts to aggressively promote Internet freedom online and I caution our government against taking any actions, such as the misguided Intellectual Property enforcement bills before Congress as we speak, that might hamstring these efforts abroad.

In addition to doing great injury to human rights, actions to restrict the free flow of information online also have serious economic repercussions. The Internet increasingly represents the shipping lane of the 21st century. Others have likened it to a digital Silk Road, ferrying electrons around the world and enabling trade in service sectors that were not too long ago considered by economists to be nontradable. It erases distance, eliminates delivery costs, and connects the smallest businesses in the most remote places with a worldwide market. Now a U.S. engineer, a German lawyer, a British banker or an Indian accountant can ply their trade anywhere in the world that has an Internet connection—and all without ever having to get on a plane and pass through a customs checkpoint. In fact, a recent McKinsey study found that the Internet accounted for 21 percent of GDP growth of mature economies over the last five years.[1]

---

[1] James Manyika and Charles Roxburgh, "The great transformer: the impact of the Internet on economic growth and prosperity," MCKINSEY GLOBAL INSTITUTE, October 2011, http://www.mckinsey.com/mgi/publications/great—transformer/pdfs/McKinsey—the—great—transformer.pdf

I. THE BENEFITS OF A TRADE APPROACH

The Internet industry is one sector where the United States enjoys a comparative advantage over the rest of the world. Despite the best efforts of other nations, no other country has been able to duplicate Silicon Valley. Besides the Internet being a major input of nearly all traditional businesses, American companies whose main purpose is to facilitate communication and make information more easily accessible are some of our biggest and fastest growing companies. Google, currently the 28th most valuable company in the world with a market valuation of $174 billion, and Facebook, whose estimated market value is $83 billion, are both more highly valued than Goldman Sachs.[2] This is big business for America, and these businesses also happen to be the tools that empower people to communicate, assemble, and organize.

Since China gets full access to United States markets in sectors where it has a competitive advantage, such as low-cost manufacturing, it is disconcerting that the United States Government has not done more to ensure that America's Internet companies get the same liberalized access to the Chinese market, a market which now has more Internet users than the entire population of the United States—and the number of Chinese Internet users is growing briskly.[3] This is an important market for our domestic Internet industry.

However, we are encouraged by the USTR's recent formal inquiry into the specifics of Chinese censorship practices. By using mechanisms available to it under the WTO, the USTR has put China in a position where it must divulge specific details about its notoriously vague censorship policies or face retaliation. As the first step of dealing with Chinese restrictions is to bring them into the light of day, this move is crucial. Although it is unlikely that enforcing trade commitments can "solve" the China censorship problem as much as freedom of expression advocates, myself included, would like, the route certainly has its advantages and provides U.S. negotiators tangible sticks and carrots that are not available in the human rights arena. Prominent human rights organizations such as Human Rights Watch have also recognized the potential benefits of pursuing a trade approach.[4]

Even though the WTO allows exceptions to its rules for matters of public morals and national security, it also requires that all regulations and restrictions be transparent, provide due process to affected parties, be the least restrictive as possible and apply equally to foreign and domestic players. As of today, China complies with none of these requirements. Furthermore, the WTO has interpreted the public morals and national security exemptions reasonably narrowly in the past, so there is even some question as to the legitimacy of much of Chinese filtering at its very core under international trade law. Even if some filtering is found permissible under trade law, forcing China "to justify each and every blockage or filtering" may dampen its enthusiasm to impose such measures.[5] At the very least, it is likely that China would have to scale back, and better document, its censorship practices.

II. CHINESE CENSORSHIP

The Chinese government censors, blocks, and discriminates against foreign-based web services and content, practices which directly or indirectly advantage domestic firms. It has repeatedly blocked sites and services, including Facebook, Flickr, Foursquare, Google and Twitter. China blocked Foursquare, a social networking service, ahead of June 4, 2010, in response to a number of users who had set their location to Tiananmen Square as a way to honor the 1989 protests.[6] Additionally, China has singled out U.S. companies for censorship even when Chinese-owned services carry the same, banned content.[7]

Even a seemingly harmless site, like photo-sharing website Flickr, has been blocked in China, while its identical clone Bababian has grown steadily

[2] Financial Times "FT Global 500 2011", http://www.ft.com/intl/reports/ft-500-2011; Ari Levy, "Facebook Valuation tops Amazon.com, trailing only Google on the Web", BLOOMBERG, http://www.bloomberg.com/news/2011-01-28/facebook-s-82-9-billion-valuation-tops-amazon-com-update1-.html

[3] In 2010, China was reported to have 420 million Internet Users. See Gao Qihui, "China's Internet Population hits 420m", CHINA DAILY, July 15, 2010, http://www.chinadaily.com.cn/china/2010-07/15/content—10112957.htm

[4] Human Rights Watch, Race to the Bottom, August 2006, page 86.

[5] Tim Wu, "The World Trade Law of Censorship and Filtering." CHICAGO JOURNAL OF INT'L LAW (2006-07).

[6] Claudine Beaumont, "Foursquare Blocked in China", THE TELEGRAPH, June 4, 2010.

[7] Simon Elegant, "Chinese Government Attacks Google Over Internet Porn", TIME, June 22, 2009.

with foreign technology and no foreign competition. Likewise, blog-hosting sites Blogger and WordPress have long been blocked in China. Instead, Chinese netizens use Tianya, the 13th-most popular site in China. Far from being a sanitized land of boring blogs about daily activities, Tianya also hosts China's largest Internet forum, a vitriolic, sensationalized, and hate-filled arena that makes Western gossip sites seem like the Economist.[8]

This double standard strongly suggests that the motivation here is protectionism rather than morals.

In addition, "Google's decision to stop self-censoring its search results in mainland China and reroute traffic through its site in Hong Kong, where mainland China's censorship rules do not apply, has come at a high cost. Its share of the Chinese search market revenue plunged to 19.6 percent in the last quarter of 2010 from 35.9 percent the year before, according to Analysys International. Chief competitor Baidu has benefited greatly from Google's fading position, increasing its share of search market revenue to 75.5 percent from 58.8 percent during the same period."[9]

China has also taken action against U.S.-based services in response to specific activities of American firms or the U.S. Government itself. For instance, in response to Congress awarding the Dalai Lama with the Congressional Gold Medal in October 2007 and the opening of a YouTube Taiwan domain, China manipulated its "Great Firewall" to redirect users entering the URL for U.S. search engines to Baidu, the Chinese search engine.[10] This is the digital equivalent of diverting business to a competitor in direct contradiction to the customer's intentions.

In addition to such direct censorship, CCIA Members report that content filtering harms the quality of service that foreign firms are able to deliver, indirectly advantaging domestic Chinese services.

For instance, China filters content and services at the international gateway as transmissions enter the country and become available to users. In filtering the services and content that enter their networks, China ensures that the foreign services available to users are degraded iterations of the service available to users in other markets. As a result, foreign service and content providers must compete with degraded products against non-filtered domestic products, and as such are disadvantaged in comparison to the domestically based competitors in those countries.

Internet censorship is part of a continuing pattern of the Chinese government using trade and regulatory policies that seek to either restrict access to Chinese markets or force foreign companies to acquiesce to Chinese government demands as the price of access. China's behavior signifies its belief that access to its markets is a coin that enables them to buy their way out of playing by the global trading system rules. From its "Indigenous Innovation" policies to its export quotas for rare earth elements, China has consistently shown a willingness to flaunt international trade rules until confronted by multiple trading partners.

III. DOMESTIC PRECEDENT

In this Commission's most recent annual report it correctly identified a troubling aspect of China's censorship regime.

> Chinese Internet regulations contain vague and broad prohibitions on content that, for example, "harms the honor or interests of the nation," "spreads rumors," or "disrupts national policies on religion." In China, the government places the burden on Internet service and content providers to monitor and remove content based on these vague standards and to maintain records of such activity and report it to the government.[11]

Pending IP enforcement legislation before the House and Senate (S. 968 and H.R. 3261) share some disturbing similarities with China's approach to centralized Internet control as pointed out by the Commission. The bills create vague standards for liability and ask private companies and Internet intermediaries to police and censor their users. When coupled with blanket immunity provisions for actions taken while attempting to comply with the legislation, this bill would encourage overbroad filtering that will remove both legal and illegal content.

[8] Jordan Calinoff, "Beijing's Foreign Internet Purge", FOREIGN POLICY, January 15, 2010, available online at <http://www.foreignpolicy.com/articles/2010/01/14/chinas—foreign—internet—purge>.

[9] John Boudreau, "Google Struggles to Succeed in China Market", SAN JOSE MERCURY NEWS, April 24, 2011.

[10] Maggie Shiels, "China Criticised Over YouTube", BBC, March 25, 2009, available online at <http://news.bbc.co.uk/2/hi/technology/7962718.stm>.

[11] Congressional-Executive Commission on China Annual Report 2011, page 58.

Although the purported goal of fighting intellectual property infringement is completely different from Chinese authoritarianism, legitimizing censorship and prior restraints on speech and enforcing it through a draconian system of DNS filtering allows China to point to our own actions to justify theirs and makes the job of our diplomats much harder. Even when attempting to achieve laudable ends, like preventing intellectual property infringement, we should not require our Internet service providers to monitor their customers' communications and maintain Internet blacklists. As a letter from over 100 law professors recently pointed out, the proposed legislation goes even further than China on some fronts.

> The Act represents a retreat from the United States' strong support of freedom of expression and the free exchange of information and ideas on the Internet. At a time when many foreign governments have dramatically stepped up their efforts to censor Internet communications, the Act would incorporate—for the first time—a principle more closely associated with those repressive regimes: a right to insist on the removal of content from the global Internet, regardless of where it may have originated or be located, in service of the exigencies of domestic law. China, for example, has (justly) been criticized for blocking free access to the Internet with its Great Firewall. But even China doesn't demand that search engines outside China refuse to index or link to other Web sites outside China. The Act does just that.[12]

We must take care not to undermine our own foreign policy and trade goals by setting bad precedent in our domestic laws.

IV. MULTILATERAL APPROACH

We highly appreciate the Commission's interest in the issue of Chinese Internet censorship and its resolve to address it. CCIA has long stated that this issue is beyond the scope of any one company or industry to deal with and that it is imperative for U.S. companies to have the support of the U.S. Government if they are to effectively compete in foreign markets where their operations are being obstructed. These companies' problems are exacerbated by the highly competitive nature of Internet-based industries. The low barriers to entry and extreme economies of scale characteristic to the Internet services industry mean that companies must constantly fight off follow-on competitors seeking to replicate their success. It is possible to rapidly create (and China has indeed created) a domestic search engine, social networking site or blogging platform. Because they can be easily replaced by a domestic alternative, U.S. companies have little bargaining power vis-&-vis countries such as China.

Of course, the situation in China bears little resemblance to a competitive market in which companies legitimately compete on the merits of their product. Indeed, Chinese censorship seems to have the added objective of clearing the competitive deck of foreign competition as the Chinese government actively promotes and protects its domestic Internet companies at their expense.

> Chinese search engine Baidu enjoys its dominant player position while competitor Google struggles with Chinese government regulatory bodies. Renren and Youku were able to grow fast while the original Facebook and Youtube had been banned in China. Thus, Chinese users didn't have options but simply chose the Chinese versions of social network and video sharing service when the world's largest services were blocked in their country.[13]

Renren ultimately availed itself upon U.S. capitals markets, conducting a "spectacular" IPO on the New York Stock Exchange where it benefited handsomely from its access to the Chinese market, while its U.S. competitor was excluded.[14] In such an environment, any ceding of market share by U.S. companies plays right into Chi-

---

[12] "Professors' Letter in Opposition to "Preventing Real Online Threats to Economic Creativity and Theft of Intellectual Property Act of 2011," July 5, 2011. http://blogs.law.stanford.edu/newsfeed/files/2011/07/PROTECT-IP-letter-final.pdf

[13] Amanda Min Chung Han, "Will Investing in Chinese Information Technology Companies be Another Tulip Speculation?", ASIA–PACIFIC BUSINESS AND TECHNOLOGY REPORT, August 8, 2011, available online at <http://www.biztechreport.com/story/1492-will-investing-chinese-information-technology-companies-be-another-tulip-speculation>.

[14] Clare Baldwin & Jennifer Saba, "Renren's Big Day, a Prelude to Facebook IPO", Reuters, May 4, 2011, available online at <http://www.reuters.com/article/2011/05/04/us-renren-ipo-idUSTRE7433HI20110504>.

nese hands, leaving China with a much more malleable and compliant Internet sector.

We would also submit that the issue is beyond the scope of any unilateral action by the United States. Instead it requires the cooperation of other like-minded countries in multilateral fora. The potential of combating Internet censorship as a trade barrier lies in the fact that the rules-based international trade system is crucial to continued Chinese growth. Characterizing censorship in the context of a system whose rules China cannot afford to blatantly ignore is likely to achieve a political response in a way that traditional human rights approaches have not. Thus, CCIA strongly supports USTR's action last month seeking detailed information regarding China's Internet restrictions and their impact on U.S. trade. What success we have had in attaining Chinese concessions on issues such as Green Dam or Indigenous Innovation have come after coordinated efforts with other trading partners such as the European Union and Japan. This underscores the importance of utilizing an official multilateral forum like the WTO, and the need to incorporate new 21st century issues such as the free flow of information into the international trade system.

V. CONCLUSION

China's Internet censorship is first and foremost a deplorable practice that perverts what should be the greatest tool for communication and freedom into a tool for an authoritarian regime's control of information and of its citizens. However, the major economic distortions of this practice also demand action under the international trade system, one that China must at least be seen as respecting due to its own dependence on trade. While from a human rights perspective, it may seem akin to going after Al Capone for tax evasion, addressing Chinese censorship as a trade barrier is a legitimate, multilateral and potentially effective approach that needs to be pursued by our government at the highest levels. As the nation that invented the Internet, and as the global standard bearer in both economic and political freedom, we must continue to lead in holding the Chinese government accountable, and we must lead by example.

————

OPENING STATEMENT OF HON. CHRIS SMITH, A U.S. REPRESENTATIVE FROM NEW JERSEY; CHAIRMAN, CONGRESSIONAL–EXECUTIVE COMMISSION ON CHINA

NOVEMBER 17, 2011

The Commission will come to order. I want to welcome all of our distinguished witnesses to this very important hearing. We really appreciate the attendance of all of our panelists and guests. It's a pleasure to welcome everyone to this important hearing on "China's Censorship of the Internet and Social Media: The Human Toll and Trade Impacts." As recent events have shown, the issue of Internet censorship has only grown in terms of importance and magnitude, and I thank the Congressional-Executive Commission on China staff for organizing a hearing on this pressing issue, and for the tremendous scholarly work they have done not only in presenting our annual report, which is filled with facts and information that is actionable, but for the ongoing work that they do to monitor the gross abuses of human rights in China.

As the Congressional-Executive Commission on China's 2011 annual human rights report demonstrates, China's leadership has grown more assertive in its violation of rights, disregarding the very laws and international standards that they claim to uphold, while tightening their grip on Chinese society. As Chinese citizens have increasingly called for freedoms and reforms, China has only strengthened its controls over many areas of society—particularly over the Internet.

While China has witnessed a boom in the popularity of social media and Internet sites, Chinese citizens that access online sites today remain under the watchful eye of the state. By some accounts, China has imprisoned more Internet activists than any other country in the world, and its Internet environment ranks among the most restrictive globally. Chinese citizens are unable to voice a range of criticism that Americans undoubtedly take for granted each day: Chinese citizens that tweet about local corruption may face the threat of abuse or harassment. Citizens that express dissatisfaction over tainted food supplies that injure children—the most vulnerable population of our society—may come to hear a knock at the door. And, citizens that voice the human desire for democracy and rights protections we value so dearly may disappear into the official custody of the state, where they face torture and incarceration.

For Chinese citizens, the line that can't be crossed is unclear. While mentions of the 1989 Tiananmen protests are surely prohibited, China's censorship remains at the whimsy of governmental agencies that seek to limit what they perceive to be any destabilizing commentary. In China, the Internet provides no transparency—and citizens must weigh their choices each time they click to send an email or press a button or post personal views online. Who can forget Shi Tao, who for merely posting information about what he is not allowed to do, with regard to Tiananmen Square, garnered a 10-year prison sentence when Yahoo! opened up their personally identifiable information and gave it to the Chinese secret police that led to his conviction. There are no lists of banned words. There are no registers of prohibited topics. In China, there is no transparency. There are only consequences, and dire ones at that.

Today, we welcome two panels that will address China's Internet censorship from two perspectives. The witnesses will not only provide personal accounts of how China's censorship affects individuals and families, but also detail how China's actions hinder the rights of U.S. businesses that seek to compete fairly in China. These panels will expose China's bold disregard for its own laws and its international obligations, specifically in terms of its controls on Internet activity and expression.

In the first panel today, we will hear personal accounts of the consequences Chinese citizens face in seeking to express their fundamental rights of expression. We will hear from a son and a pastor that have seen firsthand the anxious and unforgiving hand of China's Internet police. We will hear how the simplest calls for freedom and reforms can lead to the separation of loved ones and partition of families.

In the second panel, we will hear how China's Internet restrictions and controls not only hurt its citizens, but also hurt countries seeking to better China through international trade and cooperation. On a commercial level, China similarly lacks the kind of transparency and fairness that we expect in global trading partners. China has not only failed to comply with its WTO commitments, it has exploited our expectations to create an unlevel playing field, hurting the competitiveness of U.S. businesses and workers alike.

We recognize that the Internet and social media can and should be used to provide people with greater access to honest information and to open up commercial opportunities for businesses operating in global markets. We know that the promise of information technology can not be achieved when it is used by repressive governments to find, capture, convict, and so often torture ordinary citizens for voicing concerns publicly. Information technology can not be advanced when it involves the systemic exclusion of commercial competitors and rampant disregard for transparency and intellectual property.

China is one of the most repressive and restrictive countries when it comes to the control of the Internet and the impact goes far beyond the commercial losses for U.S. companies that want to participate in that market. There are serious human rights implications and we have seen the damage inflicted countless times through the arrest of bloggers and pro-democracy activists who have used the Internet to communicate with colleagues or disseminate views and then have been arrested. What makes this situation even worse is that sometimes it is U.S. companies, and my colleagues will recall I held the first of a series of hearings where we had Microsoft, Yahoo!, Cisco, and Google before our committee—it was my subcommittee on human rights—held up their hands and promised to tell the whole truth and nothing but, and then said they couldn't tell us what they were censoring and would not tell us how they were being complicit. Harry Wu, who is here, and has been a leader on this issue, pointed out that Cisco has so enabled the secret police to track down people using police net, and that the use of cyber police, ubiquitous throughout all of China, in order to capture the best, bravest, and smartest in China, who will bring that country to democracy if only allowed to do so.

This hearing will focus on these very important issues. We are joined by our Cochairman Sherrod Brown from Ohio who will speak and then Mr. Walz who is a ranking member, and then we will go to our witnesses.

STATEMENT OF HON. SHERROD BROWN, A U.S. SENATOR FROM OHIO; COCHAIRMAN, CONGRESSIONAL-EXECUTIVE COMMISSION ON CHINA

NOVEMBER 17, 2011

The business of the Internet and social media is changing the way the world works. Just take a look at all the smartphones in this room. It has changed the way we live, the way we do business, and the way we act as a society. It has changed the world. It has made people closer to their governments and made those governments more accountable and interactive, and in the case of the "Arab Spring," it has helped topple dictators.

The purpose of today's hearing is to shed light on the darkness of China's repressive Internet and social media censorship. It is a policy that takes a very human toll, undermining human rights reforms and freedoms of expression and speech. And it is a policy that is unfair to U.S. trade interests, especially for U.S. tech companies.

It's well-documented that Chinese officials block access to many Web sites, including this Commission's. Some sites are blocked because they are considered politically sensitive, and others for reasons that we can only guess.

China's Internet control forces private companies—including U.S. companies—to censor the Internet based on vague and arbitrary standards. Many companies are forced to operate in an opaque world that we know surprisingly little about.

This policy benefits Chinese domestic companies at the expense of companies like Facebook, Twitter, and Youtube who are completely blocked in China. Companies whose business models rely on openness and transparency—are forced to be an arm of the Chinese government or turn their backs on 1.3 billion customers.

But it isn't just Silicon Valley companies that are blocked in China. It's also Ohio companies like Graftech and Edgetech that risk having their Web sites blocked or disrupted as they try to sell their products and services to reach Chinese consumers. When U.S. companies go public with complaints about these restrictions, as Google did last year, they risk retaliation by the Chinese government for doing so. Google is a company that made the unfortunate decision to work with the Chinese government. In the end it did not work out well for them.

In the absence of meaningful competition, copycat versions of Twitter and Facebook flourish in China and raise hundreds of millions of dollars, ironically, on our capital markets. For instance, in May of this year, Renren, China's version of "Facebook," raised $743 million in an IPO listed on the New York Stock Exchange. These Chinese companies are beholden to the Chinese government and Communist Party and censorship has increased—yet they want access to our free and open society. As arms of the Chinese government, these moves should be closely scrutinized.

China now has over half a billion Internet users, more than any country in the world. Most of these Internet users are young, and far more aware of Chinese and world developments than their parents. Knowledge and openness are big threats to totalitarian regimes—we know that and the Chinese government knows that. In our country knowledge and openness are pillars of our form of government.

Take the case of outspoken dissident artist Ai Weiwei. His savvy social networking skills and unabashed criticism of the government landed him an 81-day detention at a secret location earlier this year. Now the government wants him to pay $2.4 million in alleged unpaid taxes and penalties—by Tuesday. Thousands of supporters in China have sent him money over the Internet. And Ai continues to defy government orders by using Twitter to publicize his case.

In recent years the Commission has documented a growing number of cases of political imprisonment involving the Internet. Behind each case is a story and a family.

One of those cases is Mr. Li Yuanlong. Li is a journalist who was imprisoned for two years for criticizing the Communist Party online. That's why we're so grateful that Li's son, Alex, a fellow Ohioan and a student at Bowling Green State University, is here to tell Li's story.

Last month the U.S. Trade Representative filed a request for information with the World Trade Organization on China's Internet censorship. I applaud this move as a positive first step and look forward to learning what we can do to address this pressing issue. Too much is at stake—the human toll becomes insufferable, the economic threat undermines American innovation.

China plays by its own rules because we regrettably, in this institution and in our government, let them. We cannot simply wait out the inevitable power of the Internet to move the hearts and minds of the Chinese people. We must do all we can to shine the light where free expression, thought, and commerce are too often kept in the dark.

Thank you.

○